IMAGES
of America

FORT MISSOULA

IMAGES
of America

FORT MISSOULA

Tate Jones

ARCADIA
PUBLISHING

Published by Arcadia Publishing
Charleston, South Carolina

Printed in the United States of America

Library of Congress Control Number: 2012951326

For all general information, please contact Arcadia Publishing:
Telephone 843-853-2070
Fax 843-853-0044
E-mail sales@arcadiapublishing.com
For customer service and orders:
Toll-Free 1-888-313-2665

Visit us on the Internet at www.arcadiapublishing.com

*To William Evan Jones, whose behind-the-scenes efforts to preserve
Fort Missoula's history will benefit many generations to come*

CONTENTS

ACKNOWLEDGMENTS

First, a thank-you goes to Stan Cohen, who, in the midst of numerous other historical publishing projects, took time to mentor and assist this one.

Second, gratitude is expressed to Nicole Webb of the Historical Museum at Fort Missoula and Linda Johnson. They both insured that many hitherto unpublished scenes of Fort Missoula will now be accessible to a wider audience.

Third, appreciation is given to Amy Kline of Arcadia Publishing. She has likely been through the editing process with first-time authors before and will doubtlessly apply her talents to greater projects in the future.

Fourth, I have much respect for Capt. A.E. Rothermich, US Army, and Wallace Long, previous chroniclers of Fort Missoula. Their foundation of scholarship will sustain their successors' efforts.

Finally (and excepting the author of this work), a salute goes to the staff, officers, boards, volunteers, and supporters of the Historical Museum at Fort Missoula, the Northern Rockies Heritage Center, and the Rocky Mountain Museum of Military History. Their dedication to preserving Fort Missoula's history—often with the most minimal resources at their disposal—has across the decades bequeathed Missoula one of the finest historical districts in the nation. Fort Missoula's future prospects are well on track to exceeding its colorful past.

Many images in this volume appear courtesy of the Historical Museum at Fort Missoula (HMFM), Gen. Walter Johnson's family (JF), the Montana Historical Society (MHS), the US Army (USA), the US Forest Service (USFS), the US National Archives (NA), Pictorial Histories Publishing (PHP), and the Rocky Mountain Museum of Military History (RMMMH).

INTRODUCTION

From the sight of courthouse monuments to the sound of contemporary political rhetoric, a visitor to the American West will soon absorb the triumphal image of the self-made pioneer. The farmer, rancher, miner, and even the industrialist are celebrated as solitary makers of the region's success and quality of life.

Less trumpeted is the role of the federal government, particularly the post–Civil War US Army of the frontier. The provision of quiet security and economic stimulus to the Trans-Mississippi West are not subjects amenable to popular acclaim. Between the epic of the Civil War and the struggles of the world wars, commemorations of the frontier Army are few and often overshadowed by regrets over the fates of the region's Native American cultures.

A fuller consideration of the Army's role in Western development is due and not just within the academic community. Surveying the history of Fort Missoula, Montana, can provide some opening insight into the matter while introducing to the reader a colorful and engaging progression of military units, personalities, and historical vignettes. Fort Missoula's presence connected Missoula to a larger national story, allowing a small city in a distant region to make its distinctive contributions to the American narrative.

Fort Missoula's origins in the 1870s arose from a perceived need for security by Western Montana's settlers and a desire for economic activity to be generated by an Army presence. The historical record offers scant indication that the local Salish and Kootenai offered violent opposition to the American presence, but by mid-1877, orders came forth, and two companies of the 7th Infantry under the command of Capt. Charles C. Rawn pitched their tents on the banks of the Bitterroot River.

After minimal construction, the fort's garrison unintentionally and almost immediately entered into its only Indian Wars campaign. The Nez Percé War erupted that summer in Idaho, and Chief Joseph's tribespeople began their flight into Montana. Soldiers of the 7th confronted the Nez Percé at "Fort Fizzle" and later clashed with them at the Battle of the Big Hole. The fort's troops suffered several casualties before returning to their base and resuming work on their log structures. A subsequent visit by Gen. William T. Sherman gave official assent toward expanding the military reserve to a five-company post. The 7th was relieved shortly thereafter by the US 3rd Infantry Regiment. The "Old Guard," now famed for guarding Arlington National Cemetery, spent the 1880s supervising the end of regional Native American nomadic life while simultaneously developing the area's transportation and communication systems.

In 1888, the nation's post-Reconstruction racial issues arrived in Missoula with the presence of the African American 25th Infantry. One of four post–Civil War African American regiments, the "Buffalo Soldiers" (a term applied to African American troops by Native Americans in reference to their buffalo-like appearance) received initial greetings of apathy and muted disdain from the larger white community. But the 25th's cultural and athletic contributions to Missoula life—no doubt assisted by threat of the post's termination if local complaints grew too loud—won the

African American soldiery a degree of tolerance and acceptance not often found in 19th-century America. The regiment's experimental "Bicycle Corps" received national acclaim, and upon its departure for the Spanish-American War in 1898, the unit enjoyed a rousing send-off from its Missoula hosts.

As the nation shifted its attention from frontier to overseas interests, Fort Missoula often found itself in danger of closure. But skilled political footwork among the Missoula city fathers kept the post active, if at times manned by skeletal and transient garrisons. The interest of Sen. Joseph Dixon, a confidante of Pres. Theodore Roosevelt, secured for Fort Missoula a new and substantial federal investment from 1910 to 1914. The fort's modest frame structures stood overshadowed by modern concrete construction in the Spanish Mission Revival style. The state-of-the-art infrastructure bequeathed the base a new title—the "Million Dollar Post."

After a brief sojourn as a school for Army auto mechanics during World War I, Fort Missoula resumed its wait for permanent residents. The post–Great War reorganization of the Army saw to that matter when the post's longest-serving garrison, the US 4th Infantry Regiment, took up station from 1921 to 1941. Like the Army as a whole, the 4th during the 1920s mainly served as an advanced school for officers in the absence of any larger administrative tasks. But the Great Depression of the 1930s compelled the Army to undertake supervision of a work-relief program for the nation's male youths, the federal Civilian Conservation Corps (CCC). At Fort Missoula, the 4th Regiment saw to the equipping, training, and deploying of over 40,000 corpsmen to Montana's public lands. In turn, the corpsmen's park, trail, and habitat work gave embodiment to the nation's growing resource conservation ethic.

The storms of global conflict scattered Fort Missoula's community by early 1941. The 4th deployed to Alaska, and the CCC dissolved as the corpsmen enlisted to fight foes more formidable than soil erosion and forest fires. But Fort Missoula's campus found new life as an Alien Detention Center for nationals of the Axis powers. During early 1941, the Roosevelt administration struck preemptively at Italian nationals (often of military age) docked at US ports or working within the country. Over 1,000 were interned at Fort Missoula for the duration of the United States' hostilities with Italy; initial terms of confinement eased as security concerns subsided. Given a likely welcome alternative to fighting the British in North Africa, the Italians renamed the post Bella Vista or "Beautiful View." Many found remunerative work in Western Montana prior to repatriation, and several used internment as a path to US military service and citizenship.

For some Japanese nationals with long residency in the United States, the experience proved somewhat less positive. West Coast Japanese male internees entered detention after Pearl Harbor and were confined at Fort Missoula for temporary holding, subjected to loyalty hearings conducted at the Post Headquarters. In a surreal twist, some Japanese spent their confinement constructing a golf course and creating artwork before their transfer to other US detention camps in the West and Southwest.

The internees departed by 1944, but the supercharged wartime expansion of the US Army took in large numbers of men not amenable to military strictures. Fort Missoula's confinement facilities now supported the US Disciplinary Barracks, Northwestern Branch, as the many of the war's court martial convictions arrived at the post to serve out their sentences. By 1947, the last inmates were released or sent to other military prisons, and the last active US Army use of Fort Missoula concluded. But from 1947 to the present day, Fort Missoula retained at least part-time garrisons. Troops from the Montana National Guard, the US Army Reserve, the US Marine Corps, and sailors of the US Navy Reserve utilized the legacy structures for training, storage, and deployment mobilization.

Remembered images of America have perhaps not done overall justice to the federal and Army role in the West, and more specifically to Fort Missoula's past and future impacts on its host community. The following photographic history may in some small way remedy that state of affairs.

One

SOLDIER-SETTLERS

Missoula, Montana, began its existence as a settlement named Hellgate during the Civil War years. The settlement's residents lived up to its name with their behavior during its formative period, but aspiring merchants moved the commercial focus to a site called Missoula Mills by the early 1870s. As the settler population expanded, so did somewhat inflated calls for a military presence. Editor Warren Turk of the *Missoulian* wrote the following in 1874: "A military post a necessity . . . a disturbance by some drunken Indian or an outrage by some law-defying white, may start a conflagration that will require rivers of blood and treasure to extinguish."

Missoula's political class commenced its reputation for astute lobbying, and in 1876, the War Department ordered a post built in the Missoula Valley. Capt. Charles Rawn established Fort Missoula with Companies A and I of the 7th Infantry on June 25, 1877.

As the Nez Percé War spilled over from Idaho, construction of the post took a back seat to Indian warfare during the summer of 1877. Rawn sought to intercept Nez Percé chief Joseph in late July at Lolo Canyon, but the Nez Percé peacefully outflanked and escaped his barricade at "Fort Fizzle." Rawn and the remainder of the 7th Infantry then attacked the Nez Percé farther south at the Big Hole Valley on August 9 but were driven back and besieged in one of the American West's most desperate battles. The Army awarded four Medals of Honor to Fort Missoula's garrison for the action.

The US 3rd Infantry relieved Rawn's command that autumn and remained at Fort Missoula for over 10 years. The "Old Guard" built telegraph lines, surveyed local geography, policed the Flathead Indian Reservation, and escorted Native American hunting parties to the diminishing buffalo herds east of the Rockies. These operations all received local appreciation, and by 1888, Fort Missoula achieved a measure of post-frontier permanency.

OVERVIEW OF FORT MISSOULA, C. 1910. This scene offers an approximation of Fort Missoula at the time of its 1877 establishment. The location suited easy observation of the valley junction, enhanced by nearby construction timber and a fresh water supply. In 1877, Missoula proper clustered near the bases of Mount Jumbo (left) and Mount Sentinel (center). (PHP.)

COL. JOHN GIBBON, US ARMY, C. 1877. Gibbon commanded Fort Shaw, Montana, in 1877. Troops from his 7th Infantry command deployed to begin construction of Fort Missoula. A key commander at Gettysburg and other Civil War battles, Gibbon saw extensive campaigning during the 1876 Little Big Horn expedition and the 1877 Nez Percé War. (Courtesy of Nez Percé National Historic Trail.)

1878 NONCOMMISSIONED OFFICERS' QUARTERS, C. 1973. This log building remains one of Fort Missoula's earliest surviving structures. Captain Rawn's command may have selected the sites for Fort Missoula's first structures, but the succeeding 3rd Infantry garrison accomplished most of the post's early construction. From 1879 to 1898, the fort's commissary and ordnance sergeants were housed here with their families. (PHP.)

1878 LAUNDRESSES' QUARTERS, C. 1915. This barracks building provided another component of the post's first building plan. The concentration of soldiers and the need for constant sanitary measures necessitated the presence of laundresses at many frontier posts, and this building eventually became the Laundresses' Quarters. (PHP.)

1878 POWDER MAGAZINE, C. 2000. The garrison made a priority of constructing a safe structure for munitions storage, building this magazine from mortar and sandstone quarried from nearby McCauley Butte at a cost of $485. The Montana National Guard stored explosives in the building as late as the 1950s, and soldier graffiti decorates the interior of the magazine's door. (RMMMH.)

CHIEF JOSEPH, 1877. Chief Joseph led a significant faction of Idaho's Nez Percé tribe in 1877. Disputes over appropriation of tribal lands caused friction and violence between the tribe and the settler community in the first half of 1877. Joseph's band attempted to flee Army pursuit by escaping to Montana and traveled the Lolo Trail to a point southwest of the emergent Fort Missoula. (Courtesy of Nez Percé National Historic Trail.)

FORT FIZZLE SITE, C. 1934. Capt. Charles Rawn's Fort Missoula command attempted to intercept the Nez Percé by entrenching in Lolo Canyon. After three days of nonviolent confrontation in July 1877, the Nez Percé quietly outflanked Rawn and escaped southward into the Bitterroot Valley. Rawn's outnumbered force returned to Fort Missoula. Rawn's log barricade became derisively known as "Fort Fizzle." (USFS.)

BIG HOLE NATIONAL BATTLEFIELD, 1920. Fort Missoula's garrison took part in a more serious action on August 9, 1877, when it joined Colonel Gibbon and the remainder of the 7th Infantry to attack the Nez Percé in the Big Hole Valley of Montana. The tribesmen rallied and besieged the regiment on this hillside for two days, inflicting Army casualties of 29 dead and 40 wounded. (USFS.)

GENERAL OF THE ARMY WILLIAM T. SHERMAN, C. 1877. Sherman visited Fort Missoula on an inspection tour one month after the Big Hole battle. Pleased by the fort's location and the site work accomplished to date, Sherman told the *Missoulian* that he would recommend a permanent five-company establishment for the post. (Courtesy of Nez Percé National Historic Trail.)

FORT MISSOULA PARADE GROUNDS, C. 1885. An 1880s panorama reflects the advanced state of post construction at Fort Missoula. The 3rd Infantry garrison, shown here, spent much of its time providing escorts for the now-fewer Native American expeditions to the Eastern Montana buffalo grounds. The "Old Guard" also attempted to suppress the alcohol trade on the Flathead Indian Reservation. (Courtesy of US Army Military History Institute.)

Two

MISSOULA'S
SABLE LEGIONNAIRES

The 3rd Infantry left Missoula amid considerable regret in 1888. Many Missoulians considered the officers and their families part of the social fabric, and the local newspaper covered Fort Missoula affairs with almost daily fervor. The adulation stopped when the Army announced the successor unit would be the 25th Infantry Regiment, one of four segregated African American regiments established after the Civil War. The city greeted the new arrivals with at best benign neglect in lieu of overt hostility, but over the succeeding decade, the 25th's men managed to secure a level of acceptance rarely found in 19th-century America.

The 25th's band earned a reputation for quality and soon received invitations to play at area civic events. The Buffalo Soldiers fielded accomplished "base-ballists," giving Missoula teams an entry into the growing national game. The 25th's chaplain, Rev. Theophilus G. Steward, successfully battled and belittled racial discrimination when he forced the Florence Hotel to cease its color bar. Finally, Col. Andrew Sheridan Burt of the 25th proved himself a jovial raconteur who could play a rather outsize role in local life.

The 25th deployed to police labor disputes in Idaho's Silver Valley and continued to provide law enforcement on area Indian reservations. But the luxury of peace allowed for experimentation, and the 25th won the most renown for the expeditions of its Bicycle Corps to Yellowstone National Park and St. Louis, Missouri. The 25th left in 1898 for the Spanish-American War, and Missoula turned out in force to wish the soldiers well. Colonel Burt movingly told the crowd, "Nothing would please me better than to come back to Missoula some time and spend the rest of my days, and were it not for the impending war that threatens this country, I would that this train and regiment . . . be ordered back to the beautiful little post on the Bitterroot."

COMPANY F OF THE 25TH INFANTRY. The 25th stands at attention in front of the Fort Missoula Quartermaster's Building around 1895. Four African American regiments were authorized by Congress after the Civil War. They included the 9th and 10th Cavalry Regiments, joined by the 24th and 25th Infantry Regiments. Military service offered a means of advancement for African Americans in the difficult years after Reconstruction ended, but they often found assignment

to the Army's most unhealthy and desolate posts in the Southwest. Though not immune to the temptations of soldier life, the African American troops usually met tribulation with fortitude. Desertion, alcoholism, and disciplinary problems occurred sparsely in African American units when compared to the record of white regiments. (NA.)

OFFICERS OF THE 25TH INFANTRY REGIMENT, C. 1892. The officers of the African American regiment were white, though African Americans could rise to the noncommissioned ranks. Chaplain Theophilus Gould Steward (top row, left) won esteem as a clergyman and author. In July 1894, Steward was denied entrance to the dining room of the prestigious Florence Hotel in downtown Missoula. With the full support of his superiors, he protested through the press about the Florence's discriminatory policies: "I incline to the opinion that the majority of Americans are sufficiently advanced in intelligence to distinguish between social differences and business transactions, between private prejudices and private right . . . [and that a man] ought to treat his prejudices just like he would his curs, keep them on his own premises, or muzzle them when he takes them out in public." The Florence issued an apology and welcomed Steward back. Steward went on to serve the 25th during the Spanish-American War and later wrote the memoir *Fifty Years in the Gospel Ministry*. (NA.)

A CORPORAL OF THE 25TH INFANTRY AND HIS WIFE AT FORT MISSOULA, C. 1890. Noncommissioned officers could support wives and families on Army pay, which broadened the scope of community life on post. African American noncommissioned officers resided at the top of their profession and the fort's social ladder, but promotion to the officer ranks would require future reforms. (HMFM.)

OFFICERS AND LADIES OF THE 25TH. Here, soldiers and companions enjoy boating on the Bitterroot River during the 1890s. As outdoor life in America transitioned from economic necessity to recreational desire, Army officers keenly appreciated the hunting, fishing, and scenic resources of Western Montana. (PHP.)

MARK TWAIN AT FORT MISSOULA, AUGUST 1895. The visit of humorist Mark Twain proved a highlight of the Fort Missoula social calendar on August 6, 1895. Twain is shown here on Fort Missoula's Officers' Row with Col. Andrew Burt. Although an unenthusiastic short-term Confederate volunteer during the Civil War and an antimilitarist during the years of US overseas expansion, Twain was quite taken with the post and Colonel Burt's men. Twain walked out from town toward Fort Missoula that morning and got lost, then was rescued by his tour manager and taken to the front gate. A sergeant jokingly threatened to take Twain to the guardhouse, but Twain, in kind, replied, "He preferred freedom, if you don't mind!" The 25th's officers spent the day entertaining Twain with anecdotes, leading Twain to remark, "Say boys, I haven't had one put over me as good as that since the Comstock days!" (Courtesy of Center for Mark Twain Studies, Elmira College.)

Lt. James Moss, US Army, c. 1894. The lack of conflict after the Indian wars left Army officers with few routes to promotion. Moss, an 1894 West Point graduate, sought to make his reputation by promoting the bicycle as a means of military transport. General of the Army Nelson Miles permitted him to form the Bicycle Corps within the 25th Regiment in early 1896. (PHP.)

25th Infantry Bicycle Corps, c. 1897. Moss selected around 25 volunteers and taught them to maneuver on durable Spaulding bicycles. The troops were trained to wheel about, dismount, fire, and remount with precision. Military bicycle advocates were particularly interested in freeing marching armies from the need to feed and shelter livestock. (Courtesy of University of Montana.)

BICYCLE CORPS TROOPS AT CAMP, C. 1897. After a series of test rides near Fort Missoula, Moss led his men on longer expeditions to the Mission Valley and Yellowstone National Park. The Western Montana terrain took a toll on the Spaulding bicycles, making broken chains and tire rim failure common occurrences. Moss found encouragement in his successes to date, at one point leading his troops 790 miles during 126 hours of riding. During the Yellowstone excursion, artist Frederic Remington recorded his impressions of the men: "It is heavy wheeling and pretty bumpy on the grass, where they are compelled to ride, but they managed far better than one would anticipate. . . . The physique of the black soldiers must be admired: great chested, broad shouldered, upstanding fellows with bull necks, as with their rifles thrown along their packs they straddle along." (NA.)

BICYCLE CORPS TROOPS IN ST. LOUIS, MISSOURI, JULY 24, 1897. For his tour de force, Moss's command made an epic trip from Montana to Missouri. Departing on June 14, 1897, Moss used railroad tracks on occasion as the only suitable roadbed through Eastern Montana. Moss contacted alkali poisoning in Nebraska, and his African American enlisted men encountered the unwelcoming attitudes of former Confederate sympathizers in Missouri. But a recovered Moss led his men in triumph to St. Louis's Forest Park on July 24, where the St. Louis *Post-Dispatch* reported "a running fire of cheers from the throng of pleasure-seekers that was caught up in the waiting at the Cottage [Hotel]. . . . The local cyclists made a detour and lined up . . . to let the corps pass in review." But Moss and his men returned to Fort Missoula by train, as General Miles had by now lost his interest in the experiment. The development of the internal combustion engine soon rendered the matter moot as the Army found more powerful means of troop transport. (HMFM.)

BICYCLE CORPS TROOPS IN ST. LOUIS, JULY 24, 1897. After its departure from Fort Missoula, the 25th Infantry earned a record of distinction while campaigning in Cuba and the Philippines. But in 1906, racially charged accusations arose from disturbances near the regiment's posting at Brownsville, Texas. In a controversial action, the Army discharged against their will several soldiers of the 25th. (PHP.)

MISSOULA SPANISH-AMERICAN WAR VOLUNTEERS, C. 1898. Upon the departure of the 25th for action in the Spanish-American War, local militia units used the post for predeployment training. Missoula contributed to the fight Troop F, 3rd US Volunteer Cavalry. Troop F saw no action but battled severe health problems at the disease-prone Camp Thomas, Georgia. (HMFM.)

Three

IN SEARCH OF A MISSION

A new century entailed new commitments for the US Army in the Caribbean and the Western Pacific, which left the frontier legacy posts somewhat at a disadvantage in the coming competition for appropriations. Throughout the 1900s and 1910s, Missoula politicians scrambled to keep federal largesse flowing to Fort Missoula, even at this late date citing the possibility of recurring Indian troubles.

The Army kept finding rationales to garrison the post, albeit for short tours. In succession, the 8th, 24th, 7th, 6th, 2nd, 14th, and 18th Infantry Regiments sent contingents to Fort Missoula, though often at reduced strength and sometimes as token caretaker detachments. Their short stays reduced their ties to the community, which might account for the frequent reports of soldier-on-civilian and civilian-on-soldier saloon violence during this period.

On a lighter note, Fort Missoula ushered in Missoula's air age in 1911 when it hosted the first airplane flights in Western Montana. Fort Missoula boosters found a powerful ally in Sen. Joseph Dixon (R-MT), who enjoyed a close relationship with Pres. Theodore Roosevelt and other Washington powers. Dixon secured by 1908 a large appropriation to rebuild Fort Missoula to the east of its 19th-century structures, using modern architecture and design to the utmost. This "Million Dollar Post" reflected national pride in the rise of American power and prestige as well as a desire to make military life somewhat more humane for the soldier. When the new barracks opened on December 8, 1910, the *Missoulian* reported the following: "Thick, black smoke was rolling out of the chimneys of the new buildings yesterday, indicating a warmth and comfort within which will please the soldiery mightily. The new barracks are modern in every detail, and the life of the private will be made more worth while."

The new Spanish Mission Revival buildings would wait some years for permanent residents, however. World War I called the Army's attention elsewhere, though Fort Missoula briefly served as a school for Army mechanics. The western front fell silent before Army life stirred anew at Fort Missoula.

LAUNDRESSES' QUARTERS AS OF MAY 30, 1900. Army planners mediated between the political clout of Western politicians, who wished to keep frontier legacy posts open, and the need to fund new and more relevant facilities in Cuba, Puerto Rico, and the Philippines. (PHP.)

FORT MISSOULA SOLDIERS ON PARADE, C. 1901–1903. These African American soldiers are possibly from the 24th Infantry Regiment, another of the post-Reconstruction African American units. At one point nearly resorting to gunplay with local residents over access to saloons and recreational establishments, the 24th did not enjoy the same esteem that the Missoulians gave the 25th. (PHP.)

FORT MISSOULA MESS HALL, 1900s. Though serviceable by frontier standards, the facility is clearly aged and crowded by the turn of the century. As the US Army transitioned from a low-esteem haven for the economically disadvantaged to a prestigious arm of US power, public pressure grew to improve the daily life of the American soldier. (PHP.)

FORT MISSOULA GARRISON TROOPS, 1900s. The first decade of the new century witnessed the final flourishing of an unregulated saloon row near the Buckhouse Bridge, which catered to off-duty soldiers. The combustible mix of alcohol, gambling, prostitution, and firearms kept the local court system scrambling to keep up with the bluecoats' less savory adventures. (PHP.)

FORT MISSOULA GARRISON TROOPS BUILDING RIFLE PRACTICE RANGE, 1900s. The United States owed its victories in Cuba and the Philippines more to enthusiasm and decrepit opponents than the Army's peacetime organization. Pres. Theodore Roosevelt instructed Secretary of War Elihu Root to undertake a vigorous program of military reform, including more realistic training measures. (PHP.)

OLD OFFICERS' ROW AT FORT MISSOULA, 1900s. The homes reflect an attempt by the Army to replicate a village atmosphere for its personnel, at least for the officer class. In lieu of generous financial compensation, the late-frontier Army needed to offer some benefits to its junior leadership. (Courtesy of US Army Military History Institute.)

Post Hospital, Fort Missoula, Mont.

FORT MISSOULA POST HOSPITAL, C. 1900. Frontier soldiers could at least expect access to medical care at a higher level than their civilian counterparts. However, the quality of Army surgeons could vary. A modernized hospital succeeded this building by 1915. (PHP.)

OVERVIEW OF FORT MISSOULA, 1900s. A final elegy for the frontier Army, this photograph shows the post before the deluge of early-20th-century construction. A substantial amount of acreage is still devoted to the care of Army livestock. (PHP.)

OVERVIEW OF FORT MISSOULA, C. 1912. From 1908 through 1914, Sen. Joseph Dixon of Montana shepherded a major building program at Fort Missoula. The modernity of the new structures stands in looming contrast to the old frontier buildings. Dixon reasoned that where the Army put money into a post, the permanent stationing of troops would follow. The *Missoulian* proudly proclaimed the following on January 18, 1909: "The new post is arranged along lines which will take advantage of the natural beauty of the site and also adapt the construction to the natural contour, insuring perfect drainage, an uncontaminated water supply and perfect sanitary conditions throughout. . . . When completed, the post will have no rival in the country in point of beauty and convenience." (PHP.)

FORT MISSOULA BARRACKS, 1910s. Army planners took heed of the nation's experience with military mobilization, which often required ample space for expansion or erection of temporary structures. This knowledge found incorporation into Fort Missoula's redesign. (PHP.)

FORT MISSOULA BARRACKS, 1910s. The new post buildings reflected the Spanish Mission Revival architectural style, a popular design during the 1910s. Whitewashed concrete and red tile roofs bequeathed the fort something of a colonial presidio atmosphere. (PHP.)

Fort Missoula Barracks, 1910s. Each barracks block hosted up to two infantry companies, about 200 to 250 men. The new living quarters featured running water, modern plumbing, and central heating. The period lampposts out front are no longer present, but one may be viewed today next to the Commercial Building at the Western Montana Fairgrounds. (PHP.)

Interior of Fort Missoula Barracks Squad Bay, 1936. This is the earliest known scene of the barracks' interior. Among other improvements, the design allowed the enlisted men additional natural light and air, as well as more storage for belongings. (UM.)

OVERVIEW OF FORT MISSOULA, 1910s. This scene depicts the further advancement of the post's redesign, as evidenced by the more spacious hospital to the left, the new Post Exchange in the center, and new Noncommissioned Officers' Quarters to the left. (PHP.)

NEW OFFICERS' ROW, 1911. An early stage of construction is recorded here. From 1914, Fort Missoula Officers' Row rivaled many upper-class Missoula homes in terms of comfort and modern conveniences. The post commander's residence is in the center, flanked by four captains' and majors' homes and on either end by lieutenants' multiplex housing. (PHP.)

EUGENE ELY, JUNE 1911. Missoula caught aviation fever in 1911 and wanted to see an aircraft in action. Local boosters secured the services of pilot Eugene Ely, who toured the country giving demonstrations of his Curtiss Pusher airplane. Some suggested Fort Missoula as an appropriate locale, and on June 28, 1911, soldiers laid out an impromptu landing field. (PHP.)

EUGENE ELY, JUNE 1911. Here, aviator Ely prepares for takeoff from Fort Missoula on June 28, 1911. Ely won earlier renown as the first man to fly a plane off of a naval vessel when he took off from the cruiser USS *Birmingham* in the Norfolk, Virginia, Navy Yard in November 1910. He is today honored as the first US naval aviator. (MHS.)

Eugene Ely, June 1911. He prepares for takeoff at Fort Missoula on June 28, 1911. Ely clearly used the field behind the new Officers' Row homes. However, current newspaper references report him using the post's ball field, traditionally located on the Parade Grounds. Officers' Row at this point is still awaiting a coat of whitewashing. (MHS.)

Eugene Ely, June 1911. Here, he flies over Fort Missoula on June 28, 1911. Ely's flights spurred the development of aviation in Western Montana and for communities around the nation. Ely did not live to see his legacy, dying in a plane crash at the Georgia State Fair on October 18, 1911. In 1933, Ely posthumously received the US Distinguished Flying Cross for his contribution to naval aviation. (PHP.)

THE FORT MISSOULA SALUTE GUN. Two women, one identified as Mrs. Finn, pose atop the Fort Missoula salute gun in 1917. This artillery piece served Fort Missoula for several decades. The piece is also known as a "Griffen gun" or more formally as a three-inch ordnance rifled cannon. The piece was manufactured for Union army use at Phoenixville, Pennsylvania, in 1861 and shipped to Fort Missoula in 1883. At some point, ordnance specialists modified it for use as a ceremonial salute gun, converting it to a breechloader and reducing the bore. From 1883 to 1942, the gun's blast marked reveille and retreat for the post, and it escaped the World War II scrap metal drive through private purchase by a Missoula business owner. Missoula militaria collector Hayes Otoupalik bought the cannon in 1964 and displayed it at his residence prior to donating it to the Historical Museum at Fort Missoula in 2009. The gun is now permanently installed at the historical museum's entrance. (PHP.)

FORT MISSOULA POST HOSPITAL, C. 1918. A significant gap in Fort Missoula's photographic history exists for the World War I years. Civilians were apparently discouraged from visiting, and the *Missoulian* editorialized that outsiders simply did not need to know what occurred there. The need for trained personnel apparently trumped wartime paranoia sufficiently to warrant the establishment of an Army auto mechanics' school during the conflict. Joined with an advanced academic program, this branch of the Student Army Training Corps took in 200 recruits per section for 60-day sessions. But as with many other military concentrations around the nation, Fort Missoula's activities did facilitate the introduction of the Spanish influenza virus to the locality. During October 1918, Pvts. Gerard W. Corneilissen and Norbert Gerondale both caught the Spanish flu and died, receiving burial at the Post Cemetery. At one point, nearly 125 Fort Missoula residents suffered from influenza, resulting in calls for supplies and volunteer nurses from the civilian community. Other flu deaths may have occurred among the garrison, but the total is unknown. (PHP.)

ANOTHER VIEW OF THE FORT MISSOULA POST HOSPITAL, C. 1930. Spanish influenza broke out into the larger community on October 6, 1918, when 400 Student Army Training Corps personnel visited the city on their day off. In three days, 25 new influenza cases were reported, and Missoula authorities began closing theaters, churches, schools, and other public places. Nursing sisters from St. Patrick's Hospital arrived at Fort Missoula to assist overburdened Army medical personnel. In two weeks, the number of cases grew to 500, necessitating the closure of Montana State University. Missoula police confiscated the city's bar stools to prevent congregation and infection. The pandemic eventually tapered off by mid-winter, leaving a death toll of 5,000 Montanans. In 2008, Missoula health officials began study of the Fort Missoula and city responses to the 1918 pandemic as a guide to dealing with future infectious disease outbreaks. (PHP.)

FORT MISSOULA LAUNDRESSES' QUARTERS AND POST CHAPEL, C. 1920. In contrast to other Army posts, Fort Missoula does not retain a dedicated and decorated chapel. The chapel to the left operated for some years prior to 1940, when it was subsumed in the building of a new Post Headquarters Building. Traces of the chapel can be found in what is now Building T-1. (PHP.)

INTERIOR OF THE FORT MISSOULA OFFICERS CLUB, 1926. During the post–World War I years, the Laundresses' Quarters received conversion into an officers' club. The January 24, 1926, *Sunday Missoulian* celebrated the "little log cabin as a monument to the days of our hardy forefathers. Saved from a certain death by disease and decay . . . the cabin now standing was one used as quarters by two officers and their families. . . . [During renovation,] an old 1873 Springfield rifle and bayonet . . . was found under the floor of the cabin along with 50 rounds of ammunition. The reason for this strange cache probably never will be known." (PHP.)

Four

COTTONBALERS AND CORPSMEN

World War I proved most effective in redirecting the War Department's basing priorities toward large training camps in the Sunbelt. But some of the frontier outposts remained irremovable pins in the Army's maps. Reinforced by Senator Dixon's public investments, Fort Missoula secured the tenure of the 1st Battalion of the 58th Infantry Regiment, soon by postwar reorganization to be renamed the 4th Infantry.

Relieved by the peacetime demobilization from administering large numbers of troops, officers of the US Army took advantage of this temporary lull in the global conflict. Mastering the soldier's craft became first priority as the future leaders of World War II indulged in intensive study and analysis. Social niceties also ruled in a military institution where most of the principals knew one another and their families.

The Great Depression rudely interrupted this idyll. Pres. Franklin Delano Roosevelt charged the Army to provide the nation's unemployed young men with useful activity and inaugurated the federal Civilian Conservation Corps. At Fort Missoula District CCC Headquarters, the 4th Infantry saw to the intake, supply, and deployment of over 40,000 young men to public-land projects throughout Montana. The CCC district newsletter, the *Green Guidon*, in October 1934 described the new energy encompassing Fort Missoula:

> With a new wing on the barracks which will almost double the size of the permanent quarters, comfortable winter quarters will be assured everyone. Other construction activity at Fort Missoula includes a new garage and a CCC commissary. Typists, clerks and other workers are now taking a breather for a while at Headquarters. . . . [In] the past six weeks . . . about five hundred men have been enrolled into the District. . . . We sometimes wonder who were the most confused, the veterans or the rookies.

Corpsmen engaged in reforestation, soil conservation work, wildlife refuge enhancement, and the provision of visitor amenities in the national parks and forests. But the bombs of Pearl Harbor ended the corpsmen's wilderness sojourn as the nation conscripted the "Tree Army" into a fight for larger stakes. In the meantime, Fort Missoula stood by for a unique wartime mission.

FORT MISSOULA BARRACKS AND OFFICERS' ROW, C. 1920. The US Army underwent severe contractions in manpower as it exited World War I, in line with its post-conflict experiences throughout American history. But career or long-service soldiers who remained in uniform and forsook the 1920s economic boom could rely on a measure of financial security, medical benefits, and in some cases, residency in attractive locales. Fort Missoula could offer outdoor recreation in abundance, including proximity to Glacier and Yellowstone National Parks as well as the closer amenities of the Seeley-Swan Valley, Flathead Lake, and Idaho's Clearwater drainage. Hunting and fishing opportunities abounded, and the development of wilderness lodges and dude ranches allowed the less rustic-inclined to engage in at least a sampling of wilderness life. For soldiers seeking retirement and second careers, a generally welcoming Missoula community offered the possibility of entry and integration into the civilian economy. (HMFM.)

4TH INFANTRY SQUAD IN FRONT OF FORT MISSOULA BARRACKS, C. 1925. The 4th Infantry Regiment holds an impressive lineage dating from the War of 1812. Serving Gen. Andrew Jackson at the Battle of New Orleans, the regiment repulsed British attacks from behind cotton-bale breastworks, thereafter receiving the nickname "the Cottonbalers." (HMFM.)

FORT MISSOULA 4TH INFANTRY TROOPS IN WINTER UNIFORM, C. 1925. The 4th Infantry Regiment also spent time in Mexican War service and on frontier duty in Washington Territory during the 1850s. The Cottonbalers then saw action with the Union Army of the Potomac through many of its expeditions in Virginia, Maryland, and Pennsylvania. During the imperial-era campaigns, the regiment deployed to Cuba and the Philippines. (HMFM.)

DRILL EXERCISE ON FORT MISSOULA PARADE GROUNDS, C. 1920–1925. During World War I, the 4th Infantry deployed to France by April 1918. During its tour of duty on the Western Front, the regiment fought in the Marne, St. Mihiel, and Meuse-Argonne offensives. After the Armistice, French field marshal Henri Petain decorated its colors personally with the Croix de Guerre. (HMFM.)

DRILL EXERCISE ON PARADE GROUNDS, C. 1925. Among the 4th Infantry's more notable honors is the right of its musicians to wear red piping on the chevrons of its dress uniforms, normally reserved for artillerymen. During one Mexican War battle, enemy fire killed or wounded all of the 4th's supporting artillerymen. The regiment's musicians stepped forward to man the guns. (HMFM.)

4TH INFANTRY MACHINE GUN SQUADS, C. 1925. The US Army spent the 1920s and 1930s attempting to absorb the lessons taught by combat to the British and French on the Western Front. Among them resided the critical importance of the machine gun in holding attacking infantry at bay. (HMFM.)

MACHINE GUN FOR 4TH INFANTRY'S COMPANY D DEPLOYED FOR ANTI-AIRCRAFT DEFENSE, FORT MISSOULA PARADE GROUND, C. 1937. The Model 1917 Browning gun came late to World War I but remained in US Army service through the Vietnam War. Water-cooled, the gun fired up to 600 rounds per minute. Pre–World War II variants could be transported by the disassembled cart shown here. (HMFM.)

4TH INFANTRY SQUAD IN FRONT OF FORT MISSOULA BARRACKS, C. 1925. The "Old Army" of the interwar era retained as its core long-service soldiers with significant experience. The service's disciplinary problems fell in significance after World War I due to the combination of volunteer status and enhanced military quality of life. Noncommissioned officers often received a free hand to mete out barracks-room justice, and the Great Depression reinforced attention to behavior among the lower ranks confronted with the alternative of separation in an unfriendly economic environment. Increased attention to the welfare of enlisted personnel is noted in the following October 6, 1921, *Missoula Sentinel* item: "Much interest was created yesterday among soldiers at Fort Missoula when notice was given that arrangements are now being made for the establishment of a school under the direction of Chaplain Benjamin, who has just been designated moral education and recreation officer for the post. . . . General school subjects and typewriting and stenography will be offered at the new school." (HMFM.)

US Cavalryman and Mount, c. 1925. Though America had decisively entered the era of the Model T and automotive transport by the mid-1920s, the tradition-bound Army found itself reluctant to entirely abandon animal-powered transport. (RMMMH.)

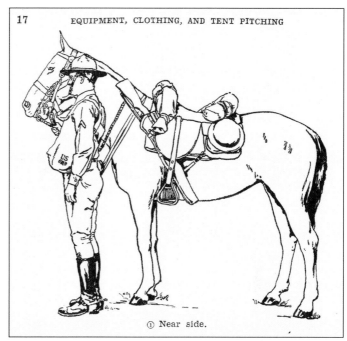

17   EQUIPMENT, CLOTHING, AND TENT PITCHING

① Near side.

Fort Missoula Mule Skinner in Army Fatigues, c. 1925. The mule did prove surprisingly resilient as a four-legged warrior during World War II. The United States supplied substantial numbers of mules and handlers to the Nationalist Chinese government during World War II for use in China's primitive interior, and US troops utilized the pack animals in North Africa, Italy, and Burma. (HMFM.)

FORT MISSOULA CHRISTMAS MENU FOR COMPANY D, 4TH INFANTRY, 1929. For many soldiers, the 1929 Yuletide likely provided the most carefree holiday for many years to come. The stock market crash of 1929 heralded the coming of the Great Depression, and the Army confronted the worsening international situation of the 1930s while battling economic constraints upon its budget and modernization program. Public disillusionment with the result of World War I joined with the lack of a clear overseas mission to hamper Army resource procurement and planning, compelling the service to run down obsolescent World War I supply stocks. Parsimony became the operative watchword until the Army could realize a means of responding to the domestic economic crisis. But the costly infrastructure in place at Fort Missoula did provide critical insurance against the post's closure, and the Missoula economy weathered the Depression with significant infusions of federal expenditures. (PHP.)

CITIZENS' MILITARY TRAINING CAMP UNIT AT FORT MISSOULA, c. 1932. The Army could raise its profile and enhance its expertise at minimal expense through provision of military summer training camps for interested young men. An outgrowth of the "Plattsburg Camps," which sought to introduce military life to an unfamiliar US public prior to World War I, the Citizens' Military Training Camps (CMTC) from 1921 through 1940 trained up to 20,000 men per year in basic military skills. In over 50 CMTC sites throughout the nation, active Army units, such as the 4th Infantry, provided instruction while also seeing to the supply and oversight for camp enrollees. Congress authorized the camps in 1920 "with a view to [cadet] employment as reserve officers and noncommissioned officers, of such warrant officers, enlisted men, and civilians as may be selected upon their own applications." The CMTC's rationale halted when active military training expanded upon the outbreak of World War II, and the program terminated in 1942. (RMMMH.)

LIEUTENANT ENGLES, 4TH INFANTRY REGIMENT, US ARMY. Engles was on temporary duty, attached to the CMTC at Fort Missoula in the summer of 1932. The quality of instruction offered by the CMTC could vary. Active officers, such as Lieutenant Engles, received higher esteem than Organized Reserve Corps trainers, who drew upon a diminishing stock of World War I–era recollections. (RMMMH.)

A REGULAR ARMY FORT MISSOULA DRILL SERGEANT. Here, a drill sergeant has been assigned to the CMTC during the summer of 1932. Noncommissioned officers in the interwar Army tended to receive a great deal of respect from enlisted men and CMTC cadets alike. Combat experience in World War I and survival of the service postwar drawdown left a cadre uniquely suited to train the soldiers required for the next round of global conflict. (RMMMH.)

DAN NELSON, SUMMER OF 1932. Nelson, a CMTC cadet and first sergeant of CMTC Company A, is pictured at Camp Maxey, Fort Missoula. The CMTC developed leadership through the formation of temporary camp military units. Nelson went on to serve in the US Army during World War II, fighting in North Africa and Europe. He survived the war and retired in Kalispell, Montana. (RMMMH.)

CMTC CADET ROBERT COOMBS, CAMP MAXEY, FORT MISSOULA, SUMMER OF 1932. The temporary Camp Maxey was named after Lt. Col. Robert Maxey, who served at Fort Missoula during the 1900s. Maxey married Missoulian Lou Knowles, the daughter of prominent local citizen Judge Hiram Knowles. Maxey died in action at the World War I Battle of Cantigny in May 1918. (RMMMH.)

POLE VAULTING AT CMTC TRACK MEET, CAMP MAXEY, FORT MISSOULA, SUMMER OF 1932. The CMTC provided summer recreational activities for its cadets in addition to military training. During 1933 and 1934, enrollment in the CMTC program fell, a trend some ascribed to the superior pay offered to young men by the Civilian Conservation Corps. The CMTC weathered numerous political storms during its existence, the most critical being the antipathy of Depression-era Americans to what many considered militarism forced on youth. Advocates of government economy also looked skeptically on the program. Congressman Ross Collins (D-MS) denounced "un-American peacetime conscription of boys, which is increasingly arousing civic and religious bodies to protest. We find they are teaching the boys [in the CMTC and ROTC] to 'serve their country' by offering them prettified social activities instead of honest military preparedness." Nonetheless, the CMTC did leave a cadre of men trained in the military arts who stood ready for duty when the United States entered World War II. (RMMMH.)

CIVILIAN CONSERVATION CORPS ENROLLEES. Martin Huggins and Ward Penkake pose on the Fort Missoula Parade Ground in 1934. The Great Depression reshaped forever the relationship of Americans with their federal government, and Fort Missoula stood at the forefront of this social change. By 1933, the nation's unemployment rate reached a critical mass, and joblessness among young urban men posed a special concern. In 1933, Pres. Franklin D. Roosevelt signed legislation creating the federal Civilian Conservation Corps. Young men could enroll in the program and receive pay, room, board, education, medical care, and a clothing allowance in exchange for work on the nation's public lands. CCC work in Montana fell under the Fort Missoula Headquarters District and the 4th Infantry. As elsewhere around the nation, the Army took care of the processing and logistical needs of the corpsmen while other federal agencies oversaw the field project. The corpsmen here are wearing surplus uniforms from the Army's stocks. (PHP.)

OVERVIEW OF FORT MISSOULA DURING THE CCC YEARS, C. 1935. A network of unimproved roads and white frame buildings marks the CCC Headquarters Complex. Old Officers' Row is still in existence, and watered lawns indicate the center of 4th Infantry activity along the barracks blocks and New Officers' Row. A separate service complex is developing to the rear of the barracks block, and the fairways of the Missoula Country Club have made their appearance. (Discussions on using part of the military reservation for a golf course took up the issue over whether Army officers would receive free playing privileges.) Some residential development is evident to the north of South Avenue, but Missoula would not really grow up to the post's boundaries until after World War II. Most of the CCC enrollees left the fort after processing, but the District Headquarters Detachment cadre maintained an ongoing presence at the post. (PHP.)

A NORTHWARD VIEW TOWARD NEW OFFICERS' ROW, 1936. The Post Exchange Building reached completion in 1906, before the Dixon-backed redesign of the campus. Now known as Building T-2, the structure is a variation on a standard Army design that incorporates neoclassical design elements and Doric columns. The building also housed a library and gymnasium. (PHP.)

ANOTHER VIEW OF CCC-ERA FORT MISSOULA, C. 1936. Over 40,000 corpsmen received processing at Fort Missoula from 1933 through 1941. About 25,000 were from Montana, but many came from urban areas for a first taste of Western life. (PHP.)

A SOUTHERN CALIFORNIA CCC ENROLLEE. Here, a corpsman arrives for duty at Fort Missoula in a Ford Model V-8 in 1934. District Headquarters at this point largely consists of a tent encampment. This corpsman would stay a few days for training and then transfer to the Ashland Ranger Station Camp in Eastern Montana. (Courtesy of Colin Hardy.)

CONSTRUCTION OF DISTRICT HEADQUARTERS BUILDING AT FORT MISSOULA, APRIL 2, 1936. The foundation at right would become Building T-316 and house CCC administrative offices through 1941. Later, the structure would serve as a battalion headquarters for the Montana National Guard and eventually as the Rocky Mountain Museum of Military History. (PHP.)

CCC Warehouse, Building T-312, Fort Missoula, c. 1936. This building supplied the numerous CCC field camps around Montana. The building later served as a training facility for the Montana National Guard and is today utilized by the University of Montana's Department of Geology to store core samples. (PHP.)

CCC Boiler Office, Building T-310, Fort Missoula, c. 2000. This cottage sits atop a large coal-fired boiler that provided heat to the CCC Headquarters Complex. During the 1950s, the Montana National Guard converted the one-room office into a caretaker's cottage large enough to house a family, a function that lasted about two decades. The building today is an exhibit hall for the Rocky Mountain Museum of Military History. (RMMMH.)

FORT MISSOULA RIFLE RANGE IN PATTEE CANYON, C. 1936. Fort Missoula troops originally honed their marksmanship in the appropriately named Target Range area adjacent to the post, but rural development made continued use problematic by 1922. Much target practice shifted to the Fort Missoula Timber Reserve in Pattee Canyon during the 1920s. (JF.)

PATTEE CANYON RIFLE RANGE, C. 1936. During the parsimonious post–Civil War years, War Department administrators limited rifle practice to save money on ammunition. But by 1936, the Army actively encouraged marksmanship competition with awards and special insignia. (JF.)

FORT MISSOULA RIFLE PRACTICE AT PATTEE CANYON, C. 1936. US soldiers of the 1930s struggled to find answers posed by several decades' developments in military technology. The American Expeditionary Force of World War I left at best theoretical answers to the difficulties of assaulting entrenchments defended by machine guns. (JF.)

FORT MISSOULA RIFLE PRACTICE AT PATTEE CANYON, C. 1936. The Springfield M1903 rifle proved a harsh teacher to recruits. One CMTC cadet recalled that "hardly a man left the firing line without a black eye, a bloody nose, a bruised cheek, a fractured jaw, or busted teeth. . . . The Springfield packed . . . a recoil of more than 2,800 feet per second, and the recoil would punish a man mercilessly." (JF.)

FORT MISSOULA RIFLE PRACTICE AT PATTEE CANYON, C. 1936. The US Forest Service acquired the Fort Missoula Timber Reserve in 1926 but allowed Army rifle practice to continue until 1940. Today, the Lolo National Forest maintains the site as the Pattee Canyon Recreation Area, and a trail system permits visitors to explore the concrete bases and earthen berms of the former training site. (JF.)

FORT MISSOULA TROOPS AT PATTEE CANYON RIFLE RANGE, C. 1936. Resolution to the infantryman's dilemma arose from the development of fast-moving armored warfare at US Army posts in the South and Southwest. Fears of a Western Front–type trench stalemate subsided. (JF.)

FORT MISSOULA SWIMMING POOL, 1936. Continued use of Fort Missoula insured increased investment in amenities, and the Army constructed a pool across from the newer Post Hospital. Here, likely a soldier's wife or CCC employee enjoys a Western Montana summer day. Note the vintage streetlamp at right. Originally erected from 1909 to 1914, a number of these lamps were removed at some point during the 1920s and reinstalled by 1933. (PHP.)

CCC ENROLLEE AT THE FORT MISSOULA SWIMMING POOL, 1936. The post's stables can be seen in the distance. Administrators likely dismantled and filled in the pool by the 1950s. A former Army training climbing tower occupies the site today. (PHP.)

VIRGINIA JOHNSON (NÉE WEISEL). Virginia Johnson rides her horse Cap near the Fort Missoula Laundresses' Quarters in September 1936. Johnson proved an accomplished author, producing, among other works, 1962's *The Unregimented General: A Biography of Nelson A. Miles.* She married Lt. Walter Johnson, who went on to achieve an impressive record of accomplishment in World War II's European theater. (JF.)

VIRGINIA JOHNSON (NÉE WEISEL) ON CAP, OVERLOOKING FORT MISSOULA, SEPTEMBER 1936. Cap was a horse of some renown, winning a competition championship during the 1930s at the Western Montana Fair and Rodeo. The Weisel family also oversaw the beginnings of the Double Arrow Guest Ranch in the Seeley-Swan Valley. (JF.)

Virginia Johnson at Fort Missoula New Officers' Row, c. 1936. Integral to the officers' homes are a number of expansive porches and front lawns. While the design may have encouraged the development of post community life, these easily monitored main entrances may have also served a control function to prevent unauthorized mixing of upper and lower ranks. (JF.)

FROM LEFT TO RIGHT, MRS. HOPPER, ROSALIE MALVIHILL, VIRGINIA JOHNSON, AND MRS. MALVIHILL CONVERSE OUTSIDE FORT MISSOULA'S NEW OFFICERS' ROW, C. **1936.** By the 1930s, the post community stood in the first rank of Missoula's social networks. Retention of an officer's commission commanded a high level of respect during the Great Depression. (JF.)

INTERIOR OF JOHNSON FAMILY QUARTERS, FORT MISSOULA, **1936.** Officers of the interwar Army enjoyed relatively secure, if small, purchasing power, complimented by a range of housing and medical benefits. For the other ranks, a different set of circumstances ruled. (JF.)

FORT MISSOULA DISTRICT CIVILIAN CONSERVATION CORPS ENROLLEES, COMPANY 954, SWAN LAKE, MONTANA, 1935. Fort Missoula corpsmen deployed to public projects throughout the state, as shown in these images saved by Joyce Agrella (pages 65 and 66). Company 954 concentrated its efforts on road building and fire suppression under the direction of the US Forest Service. (RMMMH.)

CAMP GOAT CREEK, FORT MISSOULA DISTRICT CCC COMPANY 954, 1935. After establishment of this camp near Swan Lake, the June 8, 1935, Company 954 newsletter *Primeval Recorder* commented, "The country around camp is certainly wild and beautiful—the snow capped peaks of two mountain ranges rising on either side, the massive fir, pine, cedar, and tamarack trees that make up this virgin forest, the numerous creeks untouched by human hand, all contribute to make this country the most scenic . . . ever seen." (RMMMH.)

FORT MISSOULA DISTRICT CCC ROAD BUILDING PROJECT, SWAN LAKE AREA, 1935. USFS policy during the Depression years emphasized opening up forested areas to spur local economic development through logging. The August 2, 1935, *Primeval Recorder* noted, "the construction of the Woodward Creek and Goat Creek roads has been pushed ahead a great deal this week. . . . The dozer, with Frank Timmerman operating . . . caught up with the clearing crews Monday. Melvin Freeman . . . is now running a third shift on the Woodward Creek road." (RMMMH.)

THE BUGLER

ILLUSTRATION PRODUCED FOR FORT MISSOULA DISTRICT CCC NEWSLETTER *GREEN GUIDON*, JANUARY 15, 1936. CCC administrators sought to provide constructive leisure activities for their charges as well. Camp offerings included sports, libraries, musical groups, drama productions, literary endeavors, art instruction, and outdoor recreation. (RMMMH.)

4TH INFANTRY MESS LINE, C. 1936. Members of the 4th Infantry are pictured in the mess line at McCullough Ranch during the Clarke Trophy Test March on October 28, 1936. The scenic beauty encompassing Fort Missoula likely made the baneful road marches of infantry life seem a pleasure at times. Area terrain offered a variety of training challenges. (JF.)

4TH INFANTRY COOK, C. 1936. Here, the cook carves meat for the mess line. Spoiled and inadequate food caused major problems for the Army during the imperial era, compounded by operations in mainly tropical areas. Army reforms by the 1930s addressed culinary issues to a degree. (JF.)

4TH INFANTRY OFFICERS, C. 1936. Here, from left to right, Major McConnell, Captain Wharton, and Lieutenant Williams enjoy an outdoor lunch. A CMTC newsletter, the *Camp Maxey Review*, had no qualms about satirizing Fort Missoula's officers on July 16, 1936: "You're dreaming if you've seen . . . Lt. Took with over fifteen hairs on his anterior cranial prominence . . . Captain Walker without a chaw of tobacco in his mouth . . . Lt. Marshall hot-footing it on the dance floor." (JF.)

4TH INFANTRY COOK, C. 1936. The Great Depression did not completely displace culinary refinement. A Fort Missoula Thanksgiving menu for November 1939 indicates a dinner of oyster stew, baked Virginia ham, snowflake potatoes, shrimp salad, coconut and chocolate cakes, mixed fruits and nuts, cigars, and cigarettes. (JF.)

4TH INFANTRY, CAPTAIN EPPS AT LUNCH, C. 1936. The drums of war beat again by the late 1930s, albeit for small stakes. The *Missoulian* reported this mock battle on August 22, 1937: "Regular troops of the 4th and 7th Infantry Regiments are locked in combat [near] American and Sequalitchew Lakes, according to reports from northwest army maneuver headquarters. . . . Privates were heard to remark, 'Aw, the umpires are winning this war!' " (JF.)

OFFICERS OF FORT MISSOULA'S 4TH INFANTRY ON FIELD EXERCISES, C. 1936. Note the US 3rd Infantry Division insignia on the crate. The 4th was attached to the 3rd Division, which, during World War II, fought extensively in North Africa, Italy, and Northwest Europe. (JF.)

AN EVENING ON OFFICERS' ROW, C. 1936. From left to right, Kathleen Fitzgerald, Rosalie Malvihill, Virginia Johnson, and Nina Williams socialize at Officers' Row. Johnson spent her childhood on a ranch, where she took a liking to Western history. In addition to producing several books during her literary career, she wrote articles for *US Lady*, *Western Horseman*, and the *New York Times*. (JF.)

CHRISTMAS DINNER MENU FOR CCC COMPANY 952 AT NINE MILE, MONTANA, 1936. The CCC camp near the Nine Mile Remount Depot west of Missoula provided support to national forest operations. Corpsmen rebuilt much of the depot's infrastructure, which housed and cared for the large quantity of horses and mules that the US Forest Service required for its backcountry work. (PHP.)

FORT MISSOULA POST EXCHANGE, C. 1937. Lt. Walter M. Johnson oversaw the exchange operation in this building, which today bears his name. The Post Exchange's library and gym served as centers of social life for Fort Missoula's enlisted men. The exchange store offered reasonably priced food items, sporting goods, clothing, gifts, and a variety of other items. (JF.)

SGT. H.H. HOPPLE. Hopple mans the Fort Missoula Post Exchange store on February 5, 1937. The roots of the Post Exchange system date from the late 19th century, when the War Department allowed selected traders or sutlers to set up shop within military reservations. Conflicts between public and private interests inevitably arose. In 1879, Lt. W.W. Cooke "thrashed [Fort Missoula Post Trader John McCormick] with whip over official difficulties." (JF.)

SPECIAL ORDER, FEBRUARY 5, 1937. Here, Sgt. H.H. Hopple takes a special order at the Fort Missoula Post Exchange. By 1889, the War Department moved to dissolve the post trader system and, through General Order 49, sanctioned the establishment of Post Exchanges to be administered at the discretion of the local commanding officer. (JF.)

PVT. OWEN WATSON. Here, Private Watson handles duties at the Fort Missoula Post Exchange on February 5, 1937. Prior to US entry into World War II, the War Department reorganized the exchange system into a semipublic corporation administered by both military and civilian personnel, eventually branching into offering a wide selection of luxury goods. (JF.)

Lt. Walter M. Johnson. Here, Johnson performs administrative duties at the Fort Missoula Post Exchange on February 5, 1937. A 1927 West Point graduate, Johnson supervised the planting of the post's distinctive Siberian elms. During World War II, he commanded the 117th Infantry Regiment during the critical battle for St. Lo in Normandy. Retiring as a brigadier general, he spent his final decades in Missoula with his wife, Virginia. (JF.)

Capt. John W. Scheiss, US Army Reserve, Fort Missoula District CCC, c. 1937. Scheiss's name shows up frequently in Fort Missoula's CCC-era records. He administered camps at Packers Meadow, Lolo, and Savenac Tree Nursery. CCC corpsman and later historian Bill Sharp recalled him as "a top commander." Other notable Fort Missoula officers of the CCC era included post commanders Maj. Walter Root and Col. Robert Landreth. (Courtesy of Bill Sharp.)

PVT. WALTER H. SAXTON, US ARMY, C.
1938. Stationed at Fort Missoula during
the later part of the 1930s, Saxton took an
interest in chronicling daily life at the post
through photography (pages 74 through
82). His work documenting the final
flourishing of the prewar US Army's life at
Fort Missoula now reposes at the Historical
Museum at Fort Missoula. (HMFM.)

PVT. WALTER H. SAXTON IN CLASS A
UNIFORM, C. 1938. Fort Missoula backers
scored a substantial victory in the summer
of 1938 when the post received $16,367
in Works Progress Administration
appropriations. Money funded structural
rehabilitation and the construction of a
modern headquarters building. (HMFM.)

PVT. WALTER H. SAXTON OUTSIDE OF THE FORT MISSOULA POST EXCHANGE, 1938. Maj. Gen. George A. Lynch conducted an autumn review at Fort Missoula on October 25, 1938. After receiving a 13-gun salute and reviewing an honor guard of the three infantry companies on station, Lynch inspected various post improvements and gave the fort garrison a favorable evaluation. (HMFM.)

CPL. FRANCIS PROSPER AT THE FORT MISSOULA POST EXCHANGE SODA FOUNTAIN, 1938. Prosper spent World War II fighting with the US Army's 5307th Composite Group (Provisional) in the China-Burma-India theater. Trained for long-range penetration behind Japanese lines, all members of "Merrill's Marauders" received the Bronze Star as well as the Distinguished Unit Citation. (HMFM.)

4TH INFANTRY BAND FROM FORT GEORGE WRIGHT AT FORT MISSOULA, C. 1938. Fort Wright in Spokane, Washington, provided overall headquarters for the dispersed 4th Infantry. As during the frontier era, the full regiment only assembled for special drills and maneuvers. (HMFM.)

COMPANY B, 4TH INFANTRY SQUAD ROOM, C. 1938. Fort Missoula troops responded to labor unrest with some frequency during the 19th century. But the duty grew unpopular among the active Army and found relegation to the National Guard as labor unions gained traction in American life. The interwar Army's largest domestic operation targeted the Bonus March of impoverished World War I veterans in Washington, DC, on July 28, 1932. (HMFM.)

COMPANY B, 4TH INFANTRY INSPECTION GUARD AT FORT MISSOULA BARRACKS BLOCK, C. 1938. Missoulians turned out in force for Army Day festivities on April 4, 1938. A precursor to the modern Armed Forces Day, Army Day at Fort Missoula commenced with an address by post commander Col. F.L. Whitley and a report on post improvements by Lt. Col. Roscius C. Beck. (HMFM.)

COMPANY B, 4TH INFANTRY GUARD DETAIL MOVING OUT TO MARCH AT FORT MISSOULA, C. 1938. Further Army Day 1938 proceedings included a guard mount, athletic demonstrations, open houses of garrison buildings, a retreat parade, a mess hall dinner, and an evening dance. The Missoula Rotary Club cosponsored the day's activities. (HMFM.)

GUARD HOUSE CHANGE OF GUARD, FORT MISSOULA, C. 1938. The 4th Infantry visited Fort Lewis, Washington, for maneuvers during the spring of 1939. The *Missoula Sentinel* chronicled on May 10, 1939, "Beginning Thursday, the 4th Infantry will join with the 7th Infantry in taking the field for a three-day tactical exercise, involving a dawn attack, to be followed by withdrawal under cover of darkness the following night. . . . During the past 10 days of the division concentration, the [Fort Missoula] battalion has engaged in tactical exercises and combat, and anti-aircraft firing problems . . . as part of the regimental training phase." (HMFM.)

SALUTE GUN, FORT MISSOULA, C. 1939. Some dispute exists as to whether this Model 1902 field gun or the post's Civil War–era Griffen gun fired the fort's morning and evening salutes during the 1930s. Used extensively during the 1916–1917 Mexican Punitive Expedition, the three-inch M1902 could fire explosive shells or shrapnel a maximum of 8,500 yards. The gun entered obsolescence before World War I and received relegation to stateside training. From around 1970 to 1999, a Model 1902 remained on display at the Fort Missoula main gate. (HMFM.)

WINTER FIRE DRILL, FORT MISSOULA, C. 1939. Perhaps sensing the current of global events after the 1939 German invasion of Poland, Missoula city fathers gave Fort Missoula an early Christmas gift on December 14, 1939. Title to 4,000 acres of land transferred from the Anaconda Copper Mining Company to the Fort Missoula military reservation, allowing for increased rifle and artillery training. Live-fire training eventually expanded up the side of Blue Mountain to the west of the post. This practice lasted until increased recreational use of the range area rendered military use untenable by the 1990s. Environmental cleanup of spent ordnance continued as of 2011. (HMFM.)

BUGLER IN FRONT OF FORT MISSOULA POST EXCHANGE, C. 1939. Missoulians continued the jovial game of military appropriation politics. Chamber of commerce president W.D. McCune, as recorded in the December 15, 1939, *Missoulian*, presented the new land title "with the hope that this action will warrant proper consideration for Fort Missoula to participate in future appropriations to permit further expansion and development." (HMFM.)

CONSTRUCTION OF THE RECREATION CENTER, C. 1940. The combined strength of the Civilian Conservation Corps and the 4th Infantry at Fort Missoula overwhelmed the recreational facilities of the Post Exchange and required further provision of indoor recreation. Another New Deal agency, the Works Progress Administration, undertook the task of building a large log recreation hall across from the Post Exchange Building. (HMFM.)

SERGEANT BOZO, c. 1940. As any modern dog walker can attest, animals play a large role in life at Fort Missoula. For 13 years of its tour at Fort Missoula, the 4th Infantry's Company B adopted Sergeant Bozo as its mascot. Entering service with Company B at the age of three weeks, the martial canine soon won promotion to the rank of honorary master sergeant. (HMFM.)

FORT MISSOULA FIRE TRUCK, c. 1940. The burning of coal as a heat source at Fort Missoula, combined with the proliferation of temporary wood buildings during the CCC era, required an in-house fire service. The 4th Infantry Company A's barracks received significant damage from a coal bin fire in December 1940, and fire forced the evacuation of the Post Hospital in 1941. (PHP.)

FORT MISSOULA DISTRICT CCC HEADQUARTERS DETACHMENT, MOTOR POOL, APRIL 1, 1940. For a time, the age of the horse and the age of the automobile coexisted at Fort Missoula. Missoula auto magnate H.O. Bell secured some lucrative contracts to supply the CCC with cars and trucks. (RMMMH.)

Nine Mile Remount Depot Garage (now Visitors' Center), c. 2000. Given its relatively short distance from Fort Missoula District Headquarters, CCC activity at the Nine Mile Remount Depot took on something of demonstration project status for the corps. Corpsmen constructed several depot buildings in a Cape Cod–Kentucky horse farm motif. (PHP.)

CCC Camp F-36 Drafting Department, Nine Mile Remount Depot, 1940. A majority of the CCC enrollees held an eighth-grade education or less. High school equivalency classes and vocational training offered by the corps offered training for higher-paying civilian occupations with the added benefit of producing specialists for the armed services to utilize during World War II. (PHP.)

FORT MISSOULA POST HOSPITAL AND RECREATION HALL, C. 1940. By the winter of 1940, the Works Progress Administration completed work on the new log recreation facility for the post. The construction timber came from CCC Company 1963, working in the Gallatin National Forest. Upon opening, the hall offered bowling alleys, a basketball court, a stage, kitchen, and bar. Note the bugle megaphone emplaced on the Parade Ground. (PHP.)

FORT MISSOULA RECREATION HALL, C. 1940. The Recreation Hall opened with a Golden Gloves Boxing Tournament on February 22, 1940, and received its formal inauguration on March 1, 1940. At the later event, the post Officers' Club hosted a cabaret party with entertainment by roller skaters and dance school students. The Recreation Hall enjoyed a glorious but brief existence, burning to the ground on December 7, 1946. (Courtesy of Bill Sharp.)

An Aerial view of Fort Missoula during the Final Years of the CCC, c. 1940. Tennis courts make an appearance next to the Recreation Hall, and apparently a logging and landscaping project is underway on Slevin Island on the Bitterroot River behind the hospital. The large trees marking the post landscape as of 2013 are still in their youth. (PHP.)

Another Aerial View of Fort Missoula, c. 1940. Note here the streetcar line and turnaround at the upper edge of the Fort Missoula complex. In 2012, the restored streetcar returned to the fort and is now on display at the Historical Museum at Fort Missoula. Missoula's growth is evident in the background as residential development moves toward the post. (PHP.)

Five

THE WAR COMES HOME

The advent of World War II brought to Fort Missoula some of the conflict's more unique stateside episodes.

Friction with Fascist Italy provoked the Roosevelt administration's invocation of the 1917 Espionage Act, and the US government served detention orders to Italian nationals on United States–docked ships or working within US territory. The imminent Army vacation of Fort Missoula led to creation of an Alien Detention Center (ADC) at the post. On May 9, 1941, the *Missoula Sentinel*'s Nick Mariana witnessed this scene:

> One hundred and twenty-three Italian seamen and twelve officers, from the luxury liner Count Biancamano and other ships pulled into Missoula this morning [by train]. . . . "Baggagio cui!" (baggage here) they yelled. Border patrolmen inspected all luggage. . . . Among the first exclamations was: "Che bella vista!"—(what a beautiful sight!)—and thus was a new city born. For now [they] have taken to their new location and are living in . . . "Bella Vista."

At one point, over 1,200 Italians resided at Fort Missoula, utilizing both empty barracks blocks and several temporary wood-frame structures. Eventually, the Italians took on work projects within the ADC and received some freedom to work for remuneration on local farms and in the national forests. By March 1944, the Italians were mostly repatriated to Italy, though some chose to remain and make new lives in America.

Another group experienced more duress. After Pearl Harbor, the US government interned over 80,000 US citizens of Japanese descent and over 40,000 Japanese nationals, primarily on the West Coast. From the latter group, around 1,000 adult males saw incarceration at Fort Missoula, where they underwent loyalty hearings at a courtroom within the new Post Headquarters. Some received permission to work on local farms, but the Immigration Service's primary interest lay in their transfer to other detention centers around the nation.

The Alien Detention Center officially closed on July 1, 1944, but Fort Missoula served as an Army military prison for three more years. World War II left its mark on Fort Missoula, and the question now arose as to what use a growing Missoula could make of its legacy military reservation.

ITALIAN INTERNEES AT FORT MISSOULA, C. 1941. For the Roosevelt administration, memories remained fresh of German sabotage attempts on the US mainland during World War I. The internment order applied to merchant sailors aboard United States–docked ships or Italians employed within the United States and encompassed a group that either held military reservist status or was of military age. (HMFM.)

MAIL FROM ITALY TO INTERNEE TOMMASO SANTORI AT FORT MISSOULA, 1942. The message required transit through neutral Portugal and vetting by the US Immigration and Naturalization Service (INS). The INS administered the Fort Missoula Alien Detention Center, and the US Border Patrol provided security. INS-appointed superintendent Nicholas Collaer oversaw operations at the post. (PHP.)

OVERVIEW OF FORT MISSOULA ALIEN DETENTION CENTER, C. 1941. For a time, the ADC, CCC, and 4th Infantry coexisted at Fort Missoula. But in early 1941, the 4th Infantry received orders for Alaska, and it completed its move by autumn. On Halloween Night 1941, post commander Robert E. Jones hosted a farewell party for the Army presence at the Officers' Club. (PHP.)

PERIMETER OF FORT MISSOULA ALIEN DETENTION CENTER, C. 1941. Segregated from the detention center, the Fort Missoula CCC presence rapidly wound down and disbanded after Pearl Harbor. The INS fenced off some of the post for detainee incarceration and used the barracks blocks to house interned Italian merchant navy officers. Crewmen of lesser ranks utilized a number of temporary wooden barracks on the fort's eastern grounds. (PHP.)

FORT MISSOULA BARRACKS BLOCKS DURING ALIEN DETENTION CENTER CAMP PERIOD, C. 1941. The *Missoula Sentinel* reported, "The men will have their freedom—restricted. They have been given explicit orders by Francesco La Rosa and Alessandro De Luca, second officer purser of the 'Conte Biancamano,' that they must not go beyond the iron fencing which is heavily guarded by border patrolmen and sentries." (PHP.)

DETAINEE ALFREDO CIPALATO, C. 1941. Prior to his detention, Venetian native Cipalato worked as a waiter at the Italian Pavilion of the 1939 New York World's Fair. He remained in Missoula after the war and opened the Broadway Market, marrying and raising his family in Montana. He also rented space to another detainee who stayed in Western Montana, Umberto Benedetti. (Courtesy of Northern Rockies Heritage Center.)

ITALIAN INTERNEES PARADING AT FORT MISSOULA, NOVEMBER 14, 1941. Though holding nominal allegiance to Italian dictator Benito Mussolini's Fascist government, the Fort Missoula Italian internees left a minimal record of proactive hostility toward the United States or its allies. The war began going badly for Italy from 1941 on, and many Italians turned to the belief that Mussolini's troops served mainly as cannon fodder for German operations in North Africa. (PHP.)

ITALIAN INTERNEES ON WORK PROJECT, C. 1941. Gradually, the Italians took over post maintenance functions formerly handled by the Army or the CCC. Such tasks included roads and grounds repair, blacksmithing, furniture repair, woodworking, and painting. Superintendent Collaer saw the minimal pay for such tasks and an exchange system as critical to maintaining discipline and order among the center's population. (HMFM.)

MATHEMATICS CLASS FOR ITALIAN INTERNEES, C. 1941. As during the CCC years, authorities pressed Fort Missoula into service as an educational institution. Prisoner-of-war camps later established on US soil offered a classroom program that sought to dissuade POWs from Nazi and Fascist beliefs, but the Fort Missoula internee education efforts appear to have worked toward a more academic focus. (HMFM.)

HOBBIES AND CRAFTS OF ITALIAN INTERNEES, C. 1942. Italian internees busied themselves with personal projects as well, many of which concerned nautical themes. Unfortunately, many of these creations disappeared over subsequent decades. But some reside today within the collections of the Fort Missoula museums. (HMFM.)

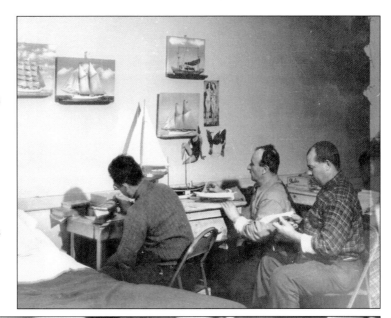

ITALIAN INTERNEE WITH SHIP MODEL, C. 1942. As described by the August 8, 1942, Helena *Montana Record-Herald*, "The happy-go-lucky Italians vary. Some make ship models, very beautiful ones. . . . There are a few gifted painters. . . . A few weeks ago the camp authorities felt they should recognize the prisoners' artistic urges. So they arranged a downtown exhibit of some of their work." (HMFM.)

Italian Internees' Soccer Game at Fort Missoula Alien Detention Center, c. 1942. A reasonable assertion can be made that the Italians first introduced "the beautiful game" to Western Montana and that Fort Missoula is indeed the birthplace of Montana soccer. Fittingly, as of 2013, plans for the adjacent Fort Missoula Regional Park call for construction of a tournament-quality youth soccer complex. (HMFM.)

Basketball Game of Italian Internees, c. 1942. The *Montana Record-Herald* noted, "Most of the day there's little to do. That's slightly irritating right now to Montana's sugar beet growers. They'd like to use some of the prisoners to harvest crops, which may have to be sacrificed because of the shortage of labor here. But the rules say 'no.'" (HMFM.)

FORT MISSOULA FIRE TRUCK DURING ALIEN DETENTION CENTER PERIOD, C. 1942. About 30 German nationals reportedly resided at the ADC during the war, formerly living in Latin American nations when their hosts declared war on the Axis. Retired University of Montana professor Carling Malouf relayed a belief to the author around 2000 that they were captured U-boat personnel turned to the Allied cause, necessitating segregation for their safety. (PHP.)

FORT MISSOULA STABLES DURING ALIEN DETENTION CAMP PERIOD, C. 1942. Although designed as an infantry post, Fort Missoula's garrisons still required substantial horse and mule livestock for officers' horses, mule supply trains, recreational riding, and other purposes. Construction of this stable occurred during the Dixon-sponsored redesign, providing another example of Spanish Mission Revival architecture. Today, the building is a laboratory for the University of Montana's Department of Biology. (PHP.)

ITALIAN INTERNEES WORKING FOR US FOREST SERVICE, C. 1943. When Italy left the side of the Axis powers, restrictions on the Italians were eased. About 360 volunteered for outside work on national forests in Montana and Idaho, undertaking some of the tasks formerly under the CCC's purview. The Italian USFS crews also undertook charitable projects such as church and orphanage repair. (USFS.)

ITALIAN INTERNEES ON AGRICULTURAL WORK RELEASE, C. 1943. Western Montana farmers got their desire, and some Italians did receive official sanction to work on local agricultural establishments. The war put severe pressure on the labor-intensive sugar beet industry, which maintained a refinement plant in Missoula. Today, the region's sugar beet farms are but a distant memory. (MHS.)

FORT MISSOULA JAPANESE INTERNEES WORKING ON POST GARDEN, C. 1942. Upon US entry into the war, the Roosevelt administration ordered the internment of about 120,000 Japanese-descent US residents. Of these, around 80,000 were US citizens and approximately 40,000 Japanese nationals. The latter did not hold US citizenship due to discriminatory naturalization laws, personal preference, or a combination thereof. From this cohort, Fort Missoula received about 1,000 men. (HMFM.)

JAPANESE INTERNEE COOK, FORT MISSOULA ALIEN DETENTION CENTER, C. 1942. The Italians and Japanese held little affinity for each other, as found by the *Montana Record-Herald*: "The Italians and the Japanese are housed in separate buildings. It was found they wouldn't even eat together, so . . . two dining rooms and two kitchens. They'll have to run [camp movies] twice, so the Axis brothers won't have to sit together." (HMFM.)

FORT MISSOULA JAPANESE INTERNEES AT BURIAL SERVICE, C. 1942. The Japanese at Fort Missoula tended to hold community leadership roles, making them of special interest to a series of Justice Department loyalty hearings. The process produced no evidence of espionage but proved stressful to the internees. Four Japanese died while in custody at Fort Missoula. (HMFM.)

JAPANESE INTERNEES' ROCK ART AT FORT MISSOULA DETENTION CENTER, C. 1942. In seeking diversions, some Japanese built a small golf course, and the *Montana Record-Herald* reported that some engage in "A curious pastime. They make gadgets from pebbles, vases, bowls, and what-nots. They'll sit alone for hours picking small pebbles from the gravel on the camp roads. . . . They work as diligently as though they were digging a tunnel to Tokyo." (MHS.)

FORT MISSOULA INTERNMENT BARRACKS, C. 1945. The West Coast Japanese largely transferred out of Fort Missoula by the early part of 1943, primarily to camps in the Mountain West and Southwest. Additional groups of internees arrived at the camp in 1943 and 1944 with the goal of eventual transfer elsewhere. By 1944, restrictions lightened sufficiently to allow Japanese-descent internees work-release and freedom of movement. (MHS.)

FORT MISSOULA INTERNMENT BARRACKS RECONSTRUCTED FOR USE AT MISSOULA COUNTY FAIRGROUNDS, C. 2000. The Fort Missoula Alien Detention Center officially closed on July 1, 1944. The Italian internees received gradual repatriation through May 1945. Local lore still recalls a memorable day at the Missoula depot when two girlfriends of an Italian internee met one another at his departure. (PHP.)

RECONSTRUCTED FORT MISSOULA INTERNMENT BARRACKS ON HISTORICAL MUSEUM AT FORT MISSOULA GROUNDS, C. 2010. Physical reminders of the Alien Detention Center started disappearing at war's end, as lumber-hungry Missoulians started dismantling the temporary structures for their own projects. Little local attention accrued to the ADC's history until the legal battle of Japanese-descent internees for compensation made national headlines during the 1980s. In the early 1990s, an attempt by the University of Montana to sell off part of the ADC site for housing development spurred local preservationists into legal and political action, and the project forestalled. A later controversy concerned an attempt by the University of Montana's biology department to expand a research facility onto the site. By 2012, the University of Montana placed a conservation easement on the ADC site and gave the Historical Museum at Fort Missoula some management authority over the property. The barracks shown above is one of the few that escaped the postwar building boom. Although not standing upon its original location, it hosts a comprehensive exhibit on the Alien Detention Center. (PHP.)

FORT MISSOULA FLAG AT HALF-STAFF. The flag flew at half-staff over the Officers' Club for the death of Pres. Franklin D. Roosevelt after April 12, 1945. The rapid growth of the US armed forces during World War II incurred significant social costs. By the third year of the war, large numbers of US soldiers proved incompatible with military discipline and found entanglement with the military legal system over offenses ranging from absence without leave to murder. To handle this surge of problem personnel, the military prison system expanded proportionally. Fort Missoula received designation as the US Disciplinary Barracks, Northwest Branch, on June 23, 1944. The facility incarcerated 2,000 inmates over a three-year period. A July 21, 1946, *Great Falls Tribune* report found, "Bull-necked, hearty Colonel J.J. France, commanding officer . . . believes in the 'pat on the back' system. He praises the prisoners, encourages them. . . . Punishment is as severe as praise. The prisoners who step out of line are slapped in 'the hole' for solitary confinement ranging from several days to a maximum of two weeks." (Courtesy of Bill Towe.)

FORMATION ON FORT MISSOULA PARADE GROUNDS OF DISCIPLINARY BARRACKS PERSONNEL, SUMMER OF 1945. Post photographs of the Disciplinary Barracks period, like those of World War I, are few. Garrison duties from 1944 to 1947 fell to the 1969th Command Service Unit of the 9th Service Command, comprising 560 officers, 576 enlisted men, and 171 civilian employees. The 1969th provided the largest Army presence recorded at Fort Missoula. (Courtesy of Bill Towe.)

FORT MISSOULA DISCIPLINARY BARRACKS PERIMETER, WINTER OF 1945. An October 20, 1944, *Missoulian* account reports, "Making his third try to escape Thursday . . . Gerald H. Jellvik, 19-year-old Everett, Washington youth, was shot to death by guards just after he succeeded clearing the high double fence of the prison compound." In another incident, an apparently mentally disturbed guard one day randomly sprayed his area with machine gun fire. (Courtesy of Bill Towe.)

Six

PRESERVING THE POST

From 1947 to the present, the military history of Fort Missoula belongs to the annals of Montana's citizen-soldiers. Troops from the Montana National Guard and US Army Reserve and sailors of the US Navy Reserve utilized the legacy structures for training, storage, and deployment. But here begins the story of Fort Missoula as a historic site.

The local historic preservation community achieved sufficient organization by the early 1970s to secure transfer of the post's core from the Army to Missoula County. This donation launched the Historical Museum at Fort Missoula, and curatorial work commenced on the frontier legacy buildings. While undertaking interpretation of general Missoula County history, HMFM often struggled financially through the 1990s. Under the leadership of Dr. Robert M. Brown, HMFM secured its future through passage of a monetary mill levy and national accreditation.

The fate of the Million Dollar Post area took center stage when the Base Realignment and Closure process sought to negotiate federal withdrawal from the complex. Another community group coalesced as the Northern Rockies Heritage Center (NRHC) and won special congressional legislation to turn Officers' Row, the Post Exchange, and much surrounding acreage over to nonprofit use. The NRHC now leases the buildings to qualifying organizations while seeking to promote diverse projects pertaining to regional education and cultural preservation.

Missoula veterans desired more specialized means of commemorating local and national military history. Negotiations with the Montana National Guard allowed for use of the remaining Civilian Conservation Corps complex, and in 2000, the Rocky Mountain Museum of Military History began restoration of the Fort Missoula District CCC Headquarters Building into its flagship display facility. The RMMMH provides exhibit galleries on all of America's conflicts from the Revolution forward, maintaining a special interest in the interwar (1919–1941) US Army.

As of 2013, Fort Missoula seems poised on the brink of even greater contributions to its namesake locality with the opening of Fort Missoula Regional Park, a recreational, natural, and historic public space promoting attention to the role of the CCC in Montana. Fort Missoula's dynamic future seems certain to surpass its illustrious heritage.

UNIDENTIFIED US ARMY OFFICER AT HIS DESK IN FORT MISSOULA POST HEADQUARTERS, 1954.
Numerous Army Reserve and Montana Army National Guard units garrisoned Fort Missoula after World War II. Army Reserve units generally reported to US Sixth Army Headquarters at the Presidio in San Francisco, California, and the 96th Regional Readiness Command in Fort Douglas, Utah. (USA.)

M.SGT. A.E. CARLSON, US ARMY, AT FORT MISSOULA POST HEADQUARTERS, 1954. Army Reserve units at Fort Missoula tended toward military engineering as a specialty, most recently serving under the aegis of the 379th Engineering Battalion. In the recent Mideast conflicts, Fort Missoula engineers deployed to Afghanistan, Iraq, and Djibouti. (USA.)

Sergeant Bankston, US Army, at Fort Missoula Post Headquarters, 1954. Montana Army National Guard units at Fort Missoula since World War II included the 443rd Field Artillery Battalion, the 154th Field Artillery Group/2nd Howitzer Battery, the 19th Special Forces Group, Headquarters and Headquarters Detachment of 6th Special Forces Battalion, Company C of 5th Special Forces Battalion, and the 1st Battalion of the 163rd Infantry (Mechanized). (USA.)

Sgt. Lewis Anderson, US Army, at Fort Missoula Post Headquarters, 1954. Indicative of the high-quality returning veterans provided to local reserve units between World War II and the Vietnam years, Bronze Star recipient Anderson served in both Korea and Vietnam. As of 2013, Montana enjoys one of the highest per capita concentrations of retired veterans in the nation. (USA.)

A VIEW OF THE SOUTHERN FORT MISSOULA BARRACKS BLOCK, 1959. Missoula hosted no local military unit from 1898 until the Montana National Guard's 443rd Field Artillery Battalion organized in the 1950s. Under the command of World War II veteran Lt. Col. M.Y. "Bo" Foster, the unit trained on the M7 Priest self-propelled howitzer. A Priest is today on display at the Rocky Mountain Museum of Military History. (USA.)

THE NORTHERN FORT MISSOULA BARRACKS BLOCK AND THE MAIN POST ENTRANCE, 1959. Troops of the 443rd deployed from Fort Missoula on April 17, 1959, responding to a lethal state prison riot at Deer Lodge, Montana. Under the command of Lieutenant Colonel Foster, the guardsmen destroyed an inmate-held guard tower with bazooka fire and stormed a rebellious cellblock. The 443rd received official thanks from Gov. Hugo Aronson. (USA.)

FORT MISSOULA BUILDING T-102, 1959. After World War II, prospects receded of an active Army unit resuming duties at Fort Missoula. Debate commenced on what further role the post could play in Missoula's economic development. The outsize maintenance needs of the campus lent the matter some urgency as the CCC and World War II temporary structures began reflecting signs of disrepair. (USA.)

UNION CONSTRUCTION COMPANY OFFICES, FORT MISSOULA, C. 1959. A temporary expedient apparently involved allowing private businesses to lease part of the military reservation. But Army correspondence found the appearance and maintenance investment of these operations less than satisfactory. A fire destroyed a large post building used by Gull Fiber Plastic Products on February 15, 1956. (USA.)

OVERVIEW OF FORT MISSOULA, C. 1959. Old Officers' Row remains but is on the verge of demolition. The main features of the CCC Headquarters Complex remain intact; however, many outbuildings are by now dismantled for scrap. A small park behind CCC Headquarters is active but will revert to a parking lot by 2013. The future grounds of the historical museum are largely bereft, but the trio of 1878 legacies—Powder Magazine, Officers' Club, and Noncommissioned Officers' Quarters—still stand sentinel. The streetcar turnaround is now absent, but the elms planted by Lt. Walter Johnson enjoy a vigorous young adulthood. Note the two rows of younger trees progressing downward from the rear of New Officers' Row. This could possibly indicate contingency planning should the post and its officer housing expand in the future. Missoula continues to grow up the Farviews hillside and toward Fort Missoula. (USA.)

COL. DONALD MACGRAIN, US ARMY, FORT MISSOULA POST COMMANDER, 1959–1961. During the 1950s, Missoula County began a campaign to secure control of Fort Missoula. In 1947, the county started leasing large portions of the base from the federal government for $9,900 per year, likely allowing the aforementioned private business operations to enter the military reservation. A proposed bond issue in 1950 to buy the entire post envisioned co-location of a "Missoula County Center" with a jail, hospital, and fairgrounds. The Missoula Chamber of Commerce lined up behind the county's aspirations. Cold War requirements shot down the county's more grandiose plans as of November 9, 1955, when the *Missoula Sentinel* reported, "Legal papers toward the return of Fort Missoula to military duty were being drawn. . . . It was announced that the Army plans to bring 2,100 men here in a weekend training program." More prophetically, Col. Joe Golden of the Army Reserve noted, "Another reason for keeping Fort Missoula intact is to preserve it as a historic site," speaking to the Missoula Rotary Club on November 11. (USA.)

VIEW OF FORT MISSOULA PARADE GROUNDS, C. 1960. As the middle of the century passed, Fort Missoula's relative isolation from urban sprawl granted its legacy structures a measure of preservation. The homes on New Officers' Row received a new lease on life when the Army chose to use them as residences for instructors in the University of Montana Reserve Officers' Training Corps program. (USA.)

FORT MISSOULA NORTHERN BARRACKS BLOCK, C. 1960. During the 1960s, the Army converted the northern barracks block into the Sgt. Ernest Veuve Army Reserve Center. Veuve served with the 4th US Cavalry in Texas and, in 1874, received the Medal of Honor for Indian Wars combat in the Staked Plains region. He arrived at Fort Missoula with the 3rd Infantry by 1877 and retired from the Army in 1880. Veuve died in Missoula in 1916. (USA.)

FORT MISSOULA POST HOSPITAL, C. 1960. Active operations at the hospital ended after closure of the Disciplinary Barracks, and by the early 1960s, the building suffered significant deterioration. In August 1962, the Missoula Women's Club acquired the hospital and four outbuildings for turnover to the Western Montana Youth Guidance Program Center. Subsequently, the Western Montana Mental Health Center established offices in the structure. (USA.)

FORT MISSOULA NONCOMMISSIONED OFFICERS' QUARTERS, C. 1960. Sadly neglected stepchildren of the Dixon-backed post redesign, these quarters are currently owned in a mothballed state by the University of Montana. By the early 1960s, the Army's policies shifted again, and it expressed interest in de-accessing additional land and buildings at Fort Missoula. (USA.)

FORT MISSOULA FIRE STATION, C. 1960. This Dixon-era structure provided fire protection and front-gate security for the post until approximately mid-century. The station now houses Lolo National Forest fire response offices. On May 1, 1962, the *Missoulian* quoted Sen. Mike Mansfield (D-MT): "The Army 'will announce plans to declare excess to its need about 500 acres of land at Fort Missoula.'" (USA.)

FORT MISSOULA WATER TOWER, C. 1960. Another Dixon-era legacy, the 1912 tower is 151 feet tall and holds 300,000 gallons. During the 1940s, the NRHC-owned tower sported a yellow-and-black checkerboard color scheme. The Fort Missoula complex is now served by the city's water system, but the tower is in the 2010s pressed into service again as the iconic symbol for Fort Missoula Regional Park. (USA.)

FORT MISSOULA OFFICERS' CLUB, C. 1960. By the 1960s, the former Laundresses' Quarters transitioned from an active-duty club to a gathering spot for military retirees. Unfortunately, this frontier legacy would not benefit from the upcoming preservation era. The *Missoulian* reported the following on November 1, 1970: "A Missoula landmark was destroyed early Monday when fire gutted a long building constructed at Fort Missoula in 1877, the year the Fort was established. . . . Although firemen fought the fire for more than three hours they were unable to save the historic Officers' Clubhouse structure. . . . [Rural fire chief Loren] Stanfield said the many remodeling partitions and false ceilings in the building made it difficult to fight the fire . . . [possibly] caused by a heat tape used on water pipes in the kitchen area." Long-term plans of the Northern Rockies Heritage Center call for rebuilding of the Officers' Club and the Recreation Hall. (USA.)

FORT MISSOULA POST CEMETERY, C. 1960. The post's final resting place dates from 1877, and burials commenced with the interment of Pvt. William Gerick on September 26, 1878. Notable residents include Indian Wars Medal of Honor recipients Henry Garland and Michael Himmelsbach, joined by the stillborn grandchild of frontier explorer Gen. John C. Frémont. Veterans of the Mexican, Civil, and Spanish-American Wars rest here, and the plot holds burials from the 7th, 3rd, 25th, 8th, 24th, 6th, 2nd, 14th, 18th, and 4th Infantry garrisons and caretaker detachments. The graves of some civilian Army employees are adjacent to that of Aati Tyrvainen, an accused World War I draft dodger who starved himself to death in the Post Hospital. A number of service personnel from the world wars and Korean and Vietnam conflicts are more recently interred. Current burials are restricted to retired career military personnel and active-duty personnel deceased while on active duty, but a newer and larger regional Western Montana State Veterans Cemetery opened nearby in 2008. (USA.)

FORT MISSOULA TROOPS ON PARADE, C. 1960. These soldiers are possibly members of the US Army Reserve 9604th Air Reserve Recovery Squadron at a University of Montana homecoming parade. As the Vietnam War advanced, the Department of Defense pressed on with plans to lower the military profile at Fort Missoula. A *Missoulian* report on November 18, 1962, detailed, "The present plan to dispose of most of Fort Missoula calls for leaving the Army with five unconnected pieces of land varying in size from one acre to 40, Colonel Elmer C. Reagor, post commanding officer, revealed. . . . The firing range is ruled out for the Marine Corps tank company because its vehicles cannot cross the old bridge over the river. . . . Ft. Missoula proper is now about 580 acres in size, about half its original area when it was a regular army post and later a prison camp." (USA.)

A WINTER SCENE ON FORT MISSOULA ROAD, C. FEBRUARY 1965. The Siberian elms planted by Lt. Walter Johnson are now in full flourish as they guard the main entrance road to the post. Concerns over suburban traffic congestion led to a reconfiguration of Fort Missoula Road during the 1970s, though the historic front entrance remains marked and preserved to an extent. (USA.)

INVITATION TO OPENING OF FORT MISSOULA RESERVE STREET NATIONAL GUARD ARMORY, NOVEMBER 12, 1977. In the mid-1970s, the National Guard moved from the CCC complex into a modern building on the fort's periphery. Maj. Gen. John. J. Womack dedicated the new headquarters in autumn 1977. Guard units stationed at the post during the decade included the Howitzer Battery and Troop G, 2nd Squadron of the 163rd Armored Cavalry. (Courtesy of Gary Lancaster.)

THE HISTORICAL MUSEUM AT FORT MISSOULA, C. 1980. The archetypal story of America's military historic sites is usually one of preservation serving as runner-up to suburban development. But in Missoula, Montana, conventional political wisdom is more often than not upended. By the 1970s, the area's historical preservation community achieved critical mass. Building on the efforts of the Western Montana Ghost Town Society to stabilize the 1878 Noncommissioned Officers' Quarters, preservationists facilitated county acquisition of the original 1877 fort acreage. Spurred by the American Revolution Bicentennial celebrations, the Historical Museum at Fort Missoula opened in rudimentary form by 1975. Locating in the 1911 Quartermaster's Storehouse, HMFM progressed from wood-stove heat and gravel-road access to a well-funded 32-acre complex offering a variety of presentations on Fort Missoula, Missoula County, and the wood-products industry. Now engaging in a long-term interpretive project on the Alien Detention Center, HMFM, as of 2013, is an accredited member of the American Alliance of Museums. (PHP.)

MOVING HELLGATE CHURCH TO THE HISTORICAL MUSEUM AT FORT MISSOULA GROUNDS, C. 1981. HMFM's grounds provide an open-air exhibit of historic regional structures and commercial equipment. St. Michael's Church is one of the few remaining physical reminders of Missoula's pioneer Hellgate settlement, being constructed by Jesuits in 1863 and subsequently receiving moves to St. Patrick Hospital and then Fort Missoula. (HMFM.)

US ARMY RESERVE MOVING SENTRY BOXES TO THE HISTORICAL MUSEUM AT FORT MISSOULA, C. 1973. As the World War II experience moved into the realm of reminisce, increased local attention grew regarding Fort Missoula's Alien Detention Center and Disciplinary Barracks years. These sentry boxes likely served during both periods, and one is now restored and present at the historical museum's front entrance. (HMFM.)

US Army Reserve Moving Hughes Garden Cabins to Historical Museum at Fort Missoula, c. 1973. The US Army continued to take an interest in Fort Missoula even as its active role at the post diminished. Army Reserve units generously provided engineering and construction aid to HMFM, and the Montana Army National Guard facilitates use of its grounds by the Rocky Mountain Museum of Military History. (HMFM.)

Green Thumb Community Assistance Workman and Friend at Noncommissioned Officers' Quarters Restoration, c. 1973. The spirits of Sergeant Bozo, Cap, and other four-legged companions live on. Fort Missoula remains a highly popular locale for Missoulians to engage in dog walking and the occasional horseback ride. Deer, ground squirrels, and ospreys also frequent the post. (HMFM.)

Green Thumb Workman during Restoration of Noncommissioned Officers' Quarters, c. 1973. Taking the lesson of the Officers' Club's fate seriously, substantial efforts are allocated to the preservation of Fort Missoula's remaining 1878 legacy structures. The Historical Museum at Fort Missoula holds responsibility for the Noncommissioned Officers' Quarters, and the Northern Rockies Heritage Center and the Rocky Mountain Museum of Military History share oversight of the Powder Magazine. (HMFM.)

Fort Missoula Noncommissioned Officers' Quarters Restoration, c. 1973. As of 2013, the Noncommissioned Officers' Quarters are stabilized and fit for public use. The residence opens on occasion for living-history demonstrations and for historical museum book-sale fundraisers during the Fourth of July. The Historical Museum at Fort Missoula plans further interpretation in the building of 19th-century military life and Fort Missoula's frontier years. (HMFM.)

FORT MISSOULA POST EXCHANGE, C. 2000. The Post Exchange Building became the Post Headquarters Building as of the 1960s, when the Army's administrative needs lessened. For a time, it hosted a US Navy Reserve unit attached to the San Diego–based frigate USS *Reasoner*. By 1998, the Post Exchange, Officers' Row, and other assets received transfer to the Northern Rockies Heritage Center. (PHP.)

FORT MISSOULA COMMANDING OFFICER'S QUARTERS, C. 1999. The NRHC received a congressional mandate to use the Million Dollar Post area for educational promotion of the region's historical and cultural legacies. The buildings are leased to qualifying organizations, and all proceeds are utilized for the nonprofit NRHC's maintenance and programming expenditures. (NRHC.)

RETIRED GENERAL FOSTER, US ARMY, C. 2003. A graduate of Yale who hitchhiked to Montana for a Forest Service job, M.Y. "Bo" Foster began his military career in the final days of the horse artillery during the 1930s. During World War II, he flew an artillery liaison plane for the US 36th Division in Europe, guarding German Luftwaffe chief Hermann Goering after the collapse of the Third Reich. (RMMMH.)

GENERAL FOSTER AT OPENING OF ROCKY MOUNTAIN MUSEUM OF MILITARY HISTORY, MAY 26, 2003. During the 1950s, Foster began National Guard operations at Fort Missoula and rose to the rank of brigadier general. In later life, he received the French Legion of Merit and served as the founding president of the Rocky Mountain Museum of Military History. (RMMMH.)

THE ROCKY MOUNTAIN MUSEUM OF MILITARY HISTORY, FORT MISSOULA, C. 2009. Chartered in 1989, the RMMMH seeks to promote the commemoration and study of the US armed forces and holds a special interest in the interwar (1919–1941) US Army. Restoration commenced on the former Fort Missoula District CCC Headquarters Building T-316 in 2000. The RMMMH renamed the structure after US Army technical sergeant Laverne Parrish, a posthumous World War II Medal of Honor recipient from Ronan, Montana. As of 2013, the museum offers a variety of indoor galleries covering most aspects of US military history, as well as a substantial research library and ongoing programs on military heritage topics. Outdoor displays include a UH-1H Huey attack helicopter flown in Vietnam and an M7 self-propelled howitzer of World War II vintage, the latter used by Building T-316's own 443rd Field Artillery Battalion during the 1950s. The museum is co-located by special arrangement with the Montana National Guard, which also administers Building T-316 and the 1878 Powder Magazine. (RMMMH.)

WORLD WAR I FRENCH RENAULT TANK AT **RMMMH, 2007.** The RMMMH serves as a regional focus for a number of military history interests. Here, RMMMH trustee Hayes Otoupalik pilots from his private collection one of three internationally remaining working models of this tank. The vehicle found national attention when featured on a History Channel documentary. (RMMMH.)

WELCOME-HOME CEREMONIES FOR SOLDIERS RETURNING FROM DEPLOYMENT AT **RMMMH, SEPTEMBER 9, 2009.** As of 2013, the military presence in Missoula centers at a joint Guard-Reserve facility west of the city. But the Montana National Guard maintains a vehicle maintenance shop at the post, and occasionally ceremonial functions recur, such as this return from Djibouti by the USAR 747th Well Drilling Detachment in 2009. (RMMMH.)

CONFEDERATED SALISH AND KOOTENAI TRIBES VETERANS WARRIOR SOCIETY AT DEDICATION OF USS *MISSOULA* EXHIBIT, ARMED FORCES DAY 2008. In 2008, the RMMMH led an effort to build a model and exhibit featuring the World War II US Navy attack transport *Missoula*. Of special interest to Western Montanans, the *Missoula* carried both the first flag to be raised by US Marines over Iwo Jima's Mount Suribachi and one of the first flag raisers, PFC Louis Charlo, of Missoula. Charlo later met his demise during the February 1945 battle. Charlo held membership in the Confederated Salish and Kootenai Tribes, and at the exhibit dedication, this cohort of Native American military veterans honored him. Fort Missoula's establishment in 1877 ostensibly intended to defend settlers against the ancestors of these tribal members. Their participation in and commemoration of the nation's defense today offers powerful testimony that history may sometimes unify rather than divide cultures. (RMMMH.)

FORT MISSOULA
ORGANIZATIONS

The following organizations welcome your support in their ongoing efforts to preserve Fort Missoula's history:

The Rocky Mountain Museum of Military History
Address: P.O. Box 7263, Missoula, Montana 59807
Phone: (406) 549-5346
Email: info@fortmissoula.org
Website: www.fortmissoula.org

The Northern Rockies Heritage Center
Address: P.O. Box 1884, Missoula, Montana 59806
Phone: (406) 728-3662
Email: director@nrhc.org
Website: www.nrhc.org

The Historical Museum at Fort Missoula
Address: Bldg. 322, Fort Missoula, Missoula, Montana 59804
Phone: (406) 728-3476
Email: ftmslamuseum@montana.com
Website: www.fortmissoulamuseum.org

Friends of Fort Missoula Regional Park
Address: P.O. Box 9092, Missoula, Montana 59807
Phone: (406) 370-6886
Email: info@fortmissoulapark.org
Website: www.fortmissoulapark.org

BIBLIOGRAPHY

The *Camp Maxey Review.* Fort Missoula: 1936.

The *CCC Green Guidon.* Fort Missoula: 1933–1941.

The CCC Company 954 *Primeval Recorder.* Swan Lake, MT: 1935.

Cohen, Stan. *Missoula County Images.* Missoula: Pictorial Histories Publishing, 1982.

———. *Missoula County Images, Volume II.* Missoula: Pictorial Histories Publishing, 1993.

The *Daily Missoulian/Missoula Sentinel/Missoulian.* Missoula: 1877–2012.

The *Great Falls Tribune.* Great Falls, MT: 1946.

Jamieson, Perry D. *Crossing the Deadly Ground: US Army Tactics, 1865–1899.* Tuscaloosa: University of Alabama Press, 1994.

Kington, Donald M. *Forgotten Summers: The Story of the Citizens' Military Training Camps, 1921–1940.* San Francisco: Two Decades Publishing, 1995.

Long, Wallace J. *The Military History of Fort Missoula.* Missoula: Friends of the Historical Museum at Fort Missoula, 1983, rev. 1991, 2005.

McDonald, James. *Fort Missoula Historic Resources.* Missoula: Fort Missoula Architectural and Historic Resources Survey, 1984.

McManus, John C. *American Courage, American Carnage: The 7th Infantry Regiment's Combat Experience, 1812 Through World War II.* New York: Forge, 2009.

Millett, Allan R. *For the Common Defense: A Military History of the United States of America.* New York: Free Press, 1984.

The *Montana Record-Herald.* Helena: 1943.

Rothermich, Capt. A.E. *Chronological Extracts from Fort Missoula Post Records.* US Army, 1933.

Sorenson, George Niels. *Iron Riders: The Story of the 1890s Fort Missoula Buffalo Soldiers Bicycle Corps.* Missoula: Pictorial Histories Publishing, 2000.

Van Valkenburg, Carol. *An Alien Place.* Missoula: Pictorial Histories Publishing, 2009.

DISCOVER THOUSANDS OF LOCAL HISTORY BOOKS
FEATURING MILLIONS OF VINTAGE IMAGES

Arcadia Publishing, the leading local history publisher in the United States, is committed to making history accessible and meaningful through publishing books that celebrate and preserve the heritage of America's people and places.

Find more books like this at
www.arcadiapublishing.com

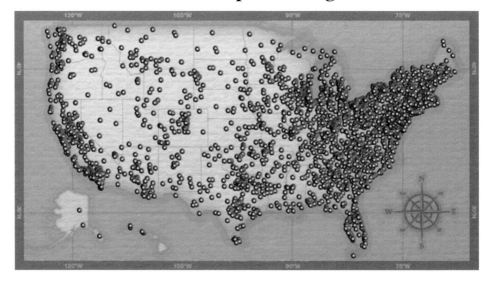

Search for your hometown history, your old stomping grounds, and even your favorite sports team.

MADE IN THE USA